Dawn Ades
was born in 1943, graduated from Oxford University
and went on to gain an MA with distinction in History of Art
from the Courtauld Institute, University of London. She is a
senior lecturer at the University of Essex and has helped to
organize the exhibitions *Dada and Surrealism Reviewed* and
Experimental Photography, both for the Arts Council. Her books
include *Dada and Surrealism* (1974), *Dali* (1982) and
Francis Bacon (1985).

WORLD OF ART

This famous series
provides the widest available
range of illustrated books on art in all its aspects.
If you would like to receive a complete list
of titles in print please write to:
THAMES AND HUDSON
30 Bloomsbury Street, London WC1B 3QP
In the United States please write to:
THAMES AND HUDSON INC.
500 Fifth Avenue, New York, New York 10110

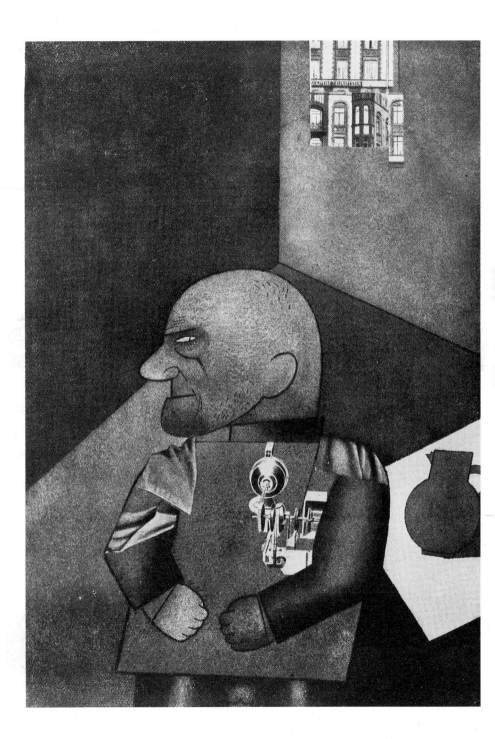

DAWN ADES

Photomontage

Revised and enlarged edition

203 illustrations

THAMES AND HUDSON

1 George Grosz *Heartfield the Mechanic* 1920

*For their generosity in giving advice and information,
and in lending material, I should like to thank Andrei
Nakov, Aaron Scharf, John Golding, Andrew Lanyon,
Peter Wollen, Joseph Rykwert, Conroy Maddox, Tim
Head, César Domela-Nieuwenhuis, Richard Sheppard,
David King, Ron Orders, Norbert Bunge, Peter
Kennard, Roger Cardinal and Andrew Brighton.*

Printed and bound in Spain by Artes Graphicas Toledo S.A.
DL.TO–895–1986

Contents

Preface to new edition

This is a revised and expanded version of *Photomontage*, first published in 1976. Since then, a considerable amount of critical and historical material has been published which has bearings on the subject of this book, in particular in relation to Dada, Constructivism and Surrealism which, in large measure, have provided the context of photomontage as I treat it here. New material has been included where appropriate, and certain sections have been revised. This is, however, a new edition, rather than a new book. The thematic structure of the original remains basically the same, as does the emphasis on photomontage in the twenties and thirties. The documentary section, which originally was placed after the text, has now been incorporated into the text with new visual material added, but the text itself has not otherwise been substantially expanded. Although more recent work is included, I cannot pretend that a representative coverage has been given to the contemporary uses of photomontage – that would have to be the subject of a different book.

CHAPTER ONE

Introduction

Manipulation of the photograph is as old as photography itself. Fox Talbot's 'photogenic drawing', one of the earliest photographic proces- 2 ses, developed during the 1830s, involved the direct contact printing of leaves, ferns, flowers, drawings, and was rediscovered and put to use with an almost infinite repertoire of objects by Man Ray, Christian 185, 184 Schad and Moholy-Nagy in their 'photograms' of the 1920s. Double 191 exposures, 'spirit photographs' (sometimes an unexpected result when an old collodion plate was imperfectly cleaned and the previous image dimly appeared on the picture), double printing and composite photo- graphs are all enthusiastically discussed in popular nineteenth-century books on 'photographic amusements' and trick photography. Cutting out and reassembling photographic images belonged on the whole to the realm of popular diversions – comic postcards, photograph albums, 3, 4 screens, military mementoes. [1]

The practice of combining photographs or photographic negatives also took place in a High Art or 'pictorial' context. One of the grandest examples was Oscar G. Rejlander's *The Two Ways of Life* (1857) which 6 was made up from more than thirty separate negatives. As Walter Woodbury described it in *Photographic Amusements*, 'Each in turn was laid upon the sensitive paper . . . and all except the part that was to be printed was covered with black velvet.' The epic scope of the final work (which measured 31 by 16 inches), its elaborate composition and alle- gorical aspirations clearly align it with classical academic painting, and Rejlander thought of his 'multiple pictures' in relation to painting: 'to show the artist how useful photography might be as an aid to their art, not only in details but in preparing what may be regarded as a most perfect sketch of their composition.' A simpler method of constructing composite pictures was that used by, for example, John Morrissey, 5 whereby ready-made pictures are re-photographed. In this composite picture of 1896, reproductions of pictures from *American Photography* were cut out, pasted together and re-photographed against a specially prepared background.

2 (*above*) William Henry Fox Talbot *Photogenic Drawing* c.1835

3 (*above right*) German postcard c. 1902

4 (*right*) *A Fine Trio* 1914: postcard of Poincaré, Tsar Nicholas and George V, allied against Germany in the First World War

5 (*opposite, above*) John P. Morrissey, composite photograph 1896

6 (*opposite, below*) Oscar G. Rejlander *The Two Ways of Life* 1857

7, 8a, 8b H. P. Robinson *Nor' Easter* from *Art Photography* 1890

9 (*opposite*) Georges Méliès, still from the film *Man with the Rubber Head* 1902

It was common practice in the nineteenth century to use combination printing to add figures to a landscape photograph, and to print in a different sky. The latter type of combination printing was used to compensate for defects in early photographic processes, for it was almost impossible, as Henry Peach Robinson explained, to obtain in one exposure both sharp foreground detail and interesting skies. 7, 8a, 8b Robinson, a painter turned professional photographer, achieved impressive meteorological effects like the storm clouds in *Nor'Easter* (from *Art Photography*, 1890) by combining two different exposures. In combination printing only a part of each negative would be used, the unused part being blanked out, while in double exposure, as Woodbury explains it, either the whole of two negatives is printed or two exposures are made on the same negative and printed.

Not all photographers regarded these practices as legitimate: the members of the Photographic Society in France were banned from exhibiting composite works.[2] The practice of combination printing lingered on, in the work of Robinson, for example, even after improvements in photographic materials rendered it no longer necessary, while trick photography retained its fascination. The young cinema was a natural site for the magic of optical tricks. Georges Méliès was one of the first film directors to experiment with trick photography.[3] In the sequence illustrated here, from *The Man with the Rubber Head* (1902), 9

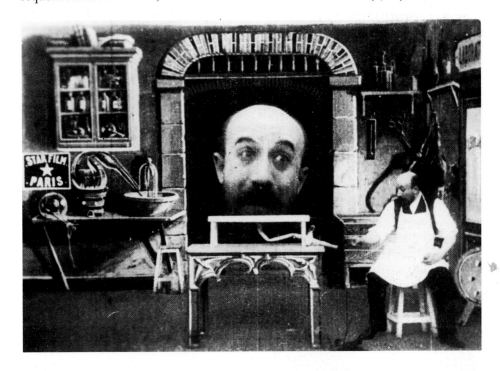

Méliès appears to blow up his own (severed) head with a pair of bellows; this was done by re-exposing the film and progressively reducing the distance between himself and the camera. In other films like *Voyage dans la lune* and *Les Quatre cent coups du Diable*, he used painted sets and constructed objects combined with photographs. But it was in a different context from that of film, or amateur or professional photography, that photomontage as it forms the subject of this book originated.

The term 'photomontage' was not invented until just after the First World War, when the Berlin Dadaists needed a name to describe their new technique of introducing photographs into their works. There are earlier, isolated examples of the use of photographs in the context of Cubist and Futurist collage. In Carrà's *French Official observing enemy movements* (1915), part of a photo of Marshal Joffre inspecting troops at the front is pasted in, in place of the head of the drawn figure. Malevich in *Woman at an advertising pillar* (1914) includes two photographic fragments. Although in these cases the pasted photographs are more frankly illustrational than most Cubist or Futurist collage, they are still incorporated into what is primarily a drawing or a painting. For the Dadaists, the photographs or fragments of photographs combined began to be the primary structuring materials of the picture. The word gained currency, therefore, in the context of an art (or anti-art) movement. The name was chosen with rare unanimity by the Berlin Dadaists, although they were later to dispute its exact historical origins within their own group. 'Seized with an innovatory zeal,' Raoul Hausmann wrote, 'I also needed a name for this technique, and in agreement with George Grosz, John Heartfield, Johannes Baader, and Hannah Höch, we decided to call these works *photomontages*. This term translates our aversion at playing the artist, and, thinking of ourselves as engineers (hence our preference for workmen's overalls) we meant to construct, to assemble [*montieren*] our works.'[4] *Montage* in German means 'fitting' or 'assembly line', and *Monteur* 'mechanic', 'engineer'. John Heartfield, perhaps the best-known practitioner of photomontage, was known as the Monteur Heartfield by the Dadaists, not simply because of his photomontages, but in recognition of an attitude, which they all shared, towards their work and its relation to existing artistic hierarchies.

The Berlin Dadaists used the photograph as a ready-made image, pasting it together with cuttings from newspapers and magazines, lettering and drawing to form a chaotic, explosive image, a provocative

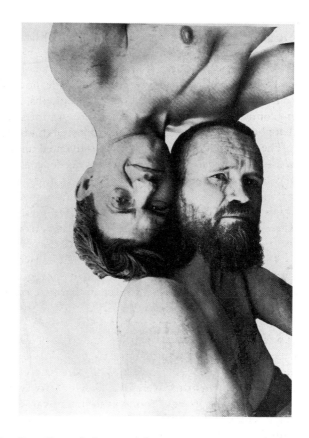

10 Raoul
Hausmann *Double
Portrait: Hausmann–
Baader* 1920

dismembering of reality. From being one element among several, the
photograph became dominant in Dada pictures, for which it was pecu-
liarly effective and appropriate material. Its use was part of the Dadaists'
reaction against oil painting, which is essentially unrepeatable, private
and exclusive. Photomontage belonged to the technological world, the
world of mass communication and photo-mechanical reproduction.[5]
When Hannah Höch said of photomontage: 'Our whole purpose was to
integrate objects from the world of machines and industry in the world
of art,'[6] I think she meant it in the sense that the materials of photomontage, particularly newspaper photographs and newsprint, were made
by mechanical processes, as well as in the iconographical sense.

14

The Russian Constructivists, who began to experiment with the
introduction of photographic material at about the same time, were to

11, 12 These are both group portraits of artists and writers associated with major reviews of the 1920s. (*left*) A page from *Novy Lef,* 1927, with, reading clockwise from top left: Tretyakov, Brik, Mayakovsky, Rodchenko, Aseev, Shklovsky, Lavinsky, Eisenstein, Pertsov, Pasternak, Zhemchuzhny, Neznamov, Kirsanov, Vertov, Stepanova, Kushner. They represent a broad-based group of 'left' artists, writers and film-makers, including Constructivists. (*right*) Montage from *La Révolution Surréaliste* 1929 with photographs of Surrealists surrounding René Magritte's painting *I Do Not See the* (Woman) *Hidden in the Forest,* clockwise from top left: Alexandre, Aragon, Breton, Buñuel, Caupenne, Eluard, Fourrier, Magritte, Valentin, Thirion, Tanguy, Sadoul, Nougé, Goemans, Ernst, Dalí. This montage parallels a similar group portrait from the first issue of *La Révolution Surréaliste;* they could be compared with the obsessive use of portraits and self-portraits in Dada photomontages. Breton, like Mayakovsky, is placed top centre in a position of dominance value photomontage for similar reasons. Also, for both the Berlin Dadaists and the Russian Constructivists, there was a need to move away from the limitations of abstraction, the dominant mode of avant-garde art, without returning to figurative painting. For both groups the photograph, with its special relation to reality, provided a solution, although, under the different conditions in which they were working, each group was to use it for different ends.

When Dada photomontage was invented it was within the context of, although in opposition to, collage. The name was chosen, clearly, to distance the two activities, and Dada recognized a very different potential in the new technique. Louis Aragon, in his essay of 1923 on Max Ernst's collages and photomontages, 'Max Ernst, peintre des illusions', sees a fundamental difference between Ernst's works and Cubist collage: 'For the Cubists, the postage stamp, the newspaper, the box of matches that the painter sticks on to his pictures, have the value of a test, an instrument of control of the reality itself of the picture. . . . With Max Ernst it is quite different . . . collage with him becomes a poetic procedure, completely opposite in its ends to Cubist collage, whose intention is purely realistic.'[7] In a later essay, 'La peinture au défi' (1930), Aragon distinguishes between the two quite distinct categories of collage: the first is that in which the stuck element is of value for its representational qualities; the second, for its material qualities. In the second, he suggests, collage operates only as an enrichment of the palette, while the first is prophetic of the direction it is to take, 'where the thing expressed is more important than the manner of expressing it, where the object represented plays the role of a word'[8] – the direction taken by Ernst.

136-8

There is little general agreement over the definition of 'photomontage' among artists and historians; the word does not appear in the OED. The Penguin English Dictionary gives 'composite picture made from several photographs; art or process of making this'. The word has tended recently to be used more in connection with photographic processes, with darkroom techniques like printing from two or more different negatives (the 'combination printing' of the nineteenth century), than with cutting up and reassembling photographs, as in the original Dada photomontages. William Rubin, for example, in his catalogue to the 1968 exhibition 'Dada, Surrealism and their Heritage' at the Museum of Modern Art in New York, stated: 'The most significant contribution of the Berlin group was the elaboration of the so-called photomontage, actually a photo-collage, since the image was not

13 Pierre Boucher, photomontage for Marcel Natkin's *Fascinating Fakes in Photography* 1939

montaged in the darkroom.'⁹ Sergei Tretyakov, on the other hand, writing about John Heartfield in 1936, took a different position: 'It is important to note that a photomontage need not necessarily be a montage of photos. No: it can be photo and text, photo and colour, photo and drawing.'¹⁰ And he quotes Heartfield himself in support: 'A photograph can, by the addition of an unimportant spot of colour, become a photomontage, a work of art of a special kind.' Although Heartfield is talking about additions to a single photograph and not of several photographs with additional elements, it is clear that it is not the technical process that interests him, but the idea, the operation that transforms the meaning of the original photograph. The definitions of Rubin and Tretyakov are really different in kind, the first assuming that photomontage is a very specific technique, the second that it must signify in a particular way. Tretyakov goes on to say: 'If the photograph, under the influence of the text, expresses not simply the fact which it shows, but also the social tendency expressed by the fact, then this is already a photomontage.'

Only in the thirties did the different users of photomontage – on the one hand amateur and professional photographers experimenting in the darkroom, and on the other hand artists who turned to the photograph, for various reasons, as a ready-made figurative element – become fully aware of each other. The 1931 edition of *Photographic Amusements*, first published in 1896, included an essay by Henry Potamkin mentioning and illustrating Moholy-Nagy, Man Ray and Bruguière. Some of the illustrations in Natkin's *Fascinating Fakes in Photography* (London, 1939), like Pierre Boucher's photomontage, show the unmistakable 13 influence of Surrealist photomontage. Natkin describes in detail photomontage by cut-out, by composition, by superposition (and superposition with mask), by superimpression, by combined superimpression and superposition, by repetition of a negative, by double printing and by combination, and also suggests, in a spirit belying the title of the book, that the ideal use of photomontage is dialectical and that above all the idea behind it must be clear.

My practice in compiling this book has been to include works 'when the imagery is predominantly photographic, whether collaged or re-photographed, rather than according to the technique'.[11] A few examples of photograms ('rayograms', 'schadographs') are also included, 184, 185, 191 because, although not strictly photomontage, they can transform relationships between familiar objects, upset the scale, suggest strange spatial effects, in a way very similar to photomontage, although finally they have more to do with chance than has the latter. There are, clearly, many other kinds of manipulated photograph, some of which were used in combination with photomontage. This book does not attempt to include all of them.

The poor quality of some of the plates in this book is due to the fact that many photomontages are made with photographs that have been cut out from magazines or newspapers and so already have a screen, and with further reproduction clarity naturally deteriorates. In certain cases the original work has disappeared (photomontages were often ephemeral) or been unavailable, and it has been necessary to reproduce from books and periodicals, which may reduce the sharpness.

14 Hannah Höch *Cut with the Cake-Knife c.* 1919

CHAPTER TWO

The Supremacy of the Message

Dada in Berlin

The invention of photomontage among the Berlin Dadaists has been claimed on the one hand by Raoul Hausmann and Hannah Höch, and on the other by George Grosz and John Heartfield. George Grosz wrote to Franz Roh when the latter was about to publish *Photo-Eye* in 1929: '. . . heartfield and I had already in 1915 made interesting photo-pasting-montage experiments. at the time we founded the grosz and heartfield concern (südende 1915). the name "monteur" I invented for heartfield, who invariably went about in an old blue suit, and whose work in our joint affair was much like mounting.'[1] Another statement by Grosz put the date at 1916, and expanded on the circumstances of the invention:

In 1916, when Johnny Heartfield and I invented photomontage in my studio at the south end of the town at five o'clock one May morning, we had no idea of the immense possibilities, or of the thorny but successful career, that awaited the new invention. On a piece of cardboard we pasted a mishmash of advertisements for hernia belts, student song books and dog food, labels from schnaps and wine bottles, and photographs from picture papers, cut up at will in such a way as to say, in pictures, what would have been banned by the censors if we had said it in words. In this way we made postcards supposed to have been sent home from the Front, or from home to the Front. This led some of our friends, Tretyakov among them, to create the legend that photomontage was an invention of the 'anonymous masses'. What did happen was that Heartfield was moved to develop what started as an inflammatory political joke into a conscious artistic technique.[2]

Hausmann on the other hand asserts that the germ of the idea was planted while he and Hannah Höch were on holiday in the summer of 1918 on the Baltic coast, where they saw in almost every house a framed coloured lithograph with the image of a soldier against a background of barracks. 'To make this military memento more personal, a photographic portrait had been stuck on in place of the head.'[3] Hannah Höch has a more precise memory, recorded by Richter in *Dada: Art and*

Anti-Art, of an 'oleograph of Kaiser Wilhelm II surrounded by ancestors, descendants, German oaks, medals and so on. Slightly higher up, but still in the middle, stood a young grenadier under whose helmet the face of their landlord, Herr Felten, was pasted in. There in the midst of his superiors, stood the young soldier, erect and proud amid the pomp and splendour of this world. This paradoxical situation aroused Hausmann's perennial aggressive streak. . . .'[4] Hausmann realized immediately that he could make pictures composed exclusively of cut-up photographs, and his excitement must have been due to the idea not just of a new technique, but of a technique in which the image would *tell* in a new way.

As Hannah Höch pointed out though, the practice of photomontage, if not the name, had been familiar since childhood, part of the world of popular postcards; it also related, she felt, to the great development of photography itself during the First World War: aerial views, microscopy and radiography.[5]

None of the postcards Grosz describes has survived, but it is possible that the 'typocollage' Heartfield designed to advertise Grosz's *Kleine Grosz Mappe* resembles them. This 'typocollage' was published in *Neue Jugend* in June 1917, which was later described as 'the first Dada review' in the catalogue of the International Dada Fair in Berlin (1920) and

15 *Germany's Safeguard* 1913, a postcard marking the twenty-fifth jubilee of Kaiser Wilhelm II

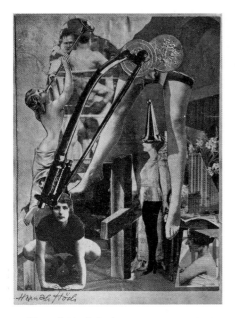

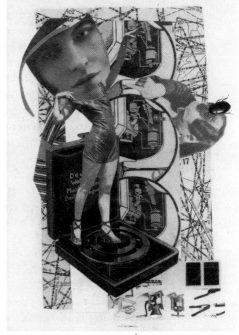

16 Hannah Höch *Dada-Ernst* 1920–1

17 Hannah Höch *Collage* 1920

contained hints of the later anarchism of Dada typography and layout. It mixes images found in printers' trays (skull and cross-bones, dancer, cigar, balloon, coffin, gramophone) among advertising slogans in a variety of type-faces. Neither this, however, nor Hausmann's collages reproduced in *Der Dada 2* (December 1919), where they are described as 'klebebild', or paste picture, used photographs as such. The catalogue of the 1969 Photomontage Exhibition at Ingolstadt states that Grosz and Heartfield first used photos in collage in 1919, and that the cover by Heartfield of the single issue of the illustrated paper *Jedermann sein eigner* 19 *Fussball* (15 February 1919) was the first dated photomontage.[6] The vignette at the top left, which gives Herzfelde the body of a football, first juxtaposed two photographs to make a new whole. The rest of the page contains a brilliant parody of a photo-gallery of political leaders, the 'beauties' of the Weimar Cabinet spread out fan-wise, with the caption 'Who is the Fairest?', reminiscent of satirical turn-of-the- 4 century postcards.

Soeben
erschienen!

20 (right) George Grosz and John Heartfield *Dada-merika* 1919

21 (far right) John Heartfield, cover for *Der Dada 3* April 1920

18, 19 'Typocollage' by John Heartfield to advertise George Grosz's lithograph portfolio, *Kleine Grosz Mappe,* from *Neue Jugend* (June 1917). It was in *Neue Jugend* that Heartfield began to form a new style of montage, out of experiments with collage and typography. *Neue Jugend* (on which Franz Jung and Grosz also collaborated) was published by Wieland Herzfelde's Malik-Verlag, founded in 1917, which moved from Berlin to Prague in 1933. It published radical literature and politics, satirical newspapers like *Jedermann sein eigner Fussball* (no. 1, 15 February 1919), and Dada works

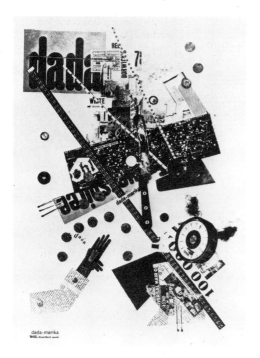

The practice of photomontage has precedence over the name. The term had its origin in the adoption of the term *montiert* or *montieren* by Grosz and Heartfield, abbreviated to 'mont.', which they stamped with their names on their works in place of a signature. *Dada-merika*, dated on the reverse 14 September 1919, and signed by Grosz alone, is stamped on the front 'grosz-heartfield mont'.[7]

20

Der Dada 3 (April 1920) has a montage cover by Heartfield, who is now regularly referred to as 'Monteur Dada', while Hausmann is the 'Dadasoph', Grosz 'Marshall' and Herzfelde 'Progress-Dada'.[8] However, the term still appears far from fixed, and there remained considerable variety in the way collages and montages were described. Grosz's montage-watercolour *Daum Marries . . .*, also reproduced in *Der Dada 3*, had the description '(Meta-Mech. constr. nach Prof. R. Hausmann)', which might translate as 'Meta-mechanical construction after Prof. Hausmann' – an ironic comment, perhaps, on the rivalry between them. The term 'photomontage' does not appear to have been in common use by the time of the International Dada Fair of May 1920. It was not used, for example, to describe Heartfield's 'Leiben und

21

Treiben in Universal-City, 12 hr. 5 mittags' (Life and Activity in Universal City at 12.05 midday), which was also used for the cover and has subsequently acquired the title 'Dada-photomontage'.[9] Portraits of Hausmann, Heartfield and Grosz by Heartfield were labelled in the catalogue 'dadaphotos'. In *Mecano* (Red), 1922, the late Neo-Dada review edited by the De Stijl artist Theo van Doesburg under his Dada pseudonym I. K. Bonset, an Ernst collage-engraving is described as 'photo-mechanical composition', and the same issue has Hausmann's

Tatlin at Home but with no descriptive label. A photomontage by Hausmann in *Mecano* (Blue) is labelled 'Construction'.

The way in which photographs were utilized in these montages or 'constructions' ran to no simple formula either; a more collage-like appearance continued side by side with the exclusive use of photographs. So, the second issue of *Der Dada* (December 1919) reproduced Hausmann's collage *Gurk*, constructed from newspaper cuttings and sliced-up woodcuts, a collage by Baader with a photograph of himself breaking through, and a fully-blown photomontage, a joint portrait of

Baader and Hausmann, with Baader's pipe 'smoking' a rose.

Grosz's and Hausmann's different accounts of the 'discovery' of photomontage both stress sources in the popular and comic arrangement of photographs, and both seized on the possibilities of signification and on the subversive potential of the medium. This is how Hausmann was to describe it much later, in his lecture at the time of the first major exhibition of photomontage in Berlin in 1931:

People often assume that photomontage is only practicable in two forms: political propaganda and commercial publicity. The first photomonteurs, the Dadaists, started from the point of view, to them incontestable, that war-time painting, post-futurist expressionism, had failed because of its non-objectivity and its absence of convictions, and that not only painting, but all the arts and their techniques needed a fundamental and revolutionary change, in order to remain in touch with the life of their epoch. The members of the Club Dada were naturally not interested in elaborating new aesthetic rules . . . But the idea of photomontage was as revolutionary as its content, its form as subversive as the application of the photograph and printed texts which, together, are transformed into a static film. Having invented the static, simultaneous and purely phonetic poem, the Dadaists applied the same principles to pictorial representation. They were the first to use photography as material to create, with the aid of structures that were very different, often anomalous and with antagonistic significance, a new entity which tore from the chaos of war and revolution an entirely new image; and they were aware that their method possessed a propaganda power which their contemporaries had not the courage to exploit . . .[10]

Towards the end of the war Berlin was a half-starved nightmare city, and there was increasing social and political chaos, which was to last until 1933; in 1918 Soviet Republics were briefly set up in several major German cities, including Berlin. Of the Berlin Dada Club, which included Huelsenbeck, Hausmann, Grosz, Wieland Herzfelde and his brother John Heartfield, Hannah Höch, Johannes Baader and, briefly, Franz Jung, only Herzfelde, Heartfield and Grosz joined the German Communist Party (KPD) in December 1918. But the group as a whole sided with the radical left wing against the middle-class republic of Ebert and Schiedemann and, after the defeat of the November Revolution, through the early months of 1919, were vociferous in their opposition. They produced many periodicals, news-sheets and pamphlets, not all of which were Dadaist, for which conventional layout seemed inappropriate, and typographical anarchy began.

In artistic terms, Dada's constant chosen enemy was Expressionism, and in singling out its inwardness and Utopianism, and the emptiness of its rhetoric, Huelsenbeck, in the first Dada Manifesto of the Berlin group in 1918, called instead for an art 'which in its conscious content presents the thousandfold problems of the day, the art which has been visibly shattered by the explosions of last week, which is forever trying to collect its limbs after yesterday's crash. The best and most extraordinary artists will be those who every hour snatch the tatters of their bodies out of the frenzied cataract of life, who, with bleeding hands and hearts, hold fast to the intelligence of their time.'[11] Photomontage perhaps comes closest to fulfilling Huelsenbeck's ideal. The visibly shattered surface of *Dada-merika,* or Heartfield's *Universal City,* is a truer image of a violent and chaotic society than, for example, *The Funeral of the Anarchist Galli,* a painting by the Futurist Carrà. And in using the very stuff of today's and yesterday's news, Dada was beginning to subvert the voice of society itself. Grosz's montage *My Germany,* for the unpublished anthology *Dadaco,* has some of the power of Heartfield's later work: Prussian soldiers are enthroned in the heart of a fat capitalist whose bland bald head sprouts snippets of the financial news. This is one of the first montages to show the inglorious association of money and war, later to be a constant theme with Heartfield.

The connection between militarism and capitalism, persistent basis for Grosz's attack on the Weimar Republic, was explored by him in a number of lithographs and drawings. In 'The communists are dying and the foreign exchange rate goes up' from *Gott mit uns,* a collection of

23 Page from trial proofs of the unpublished anthology *Dadaco* 1920

24 George Grosz *My Germany* from *Dadaco* 1920

lithographs of 1920, the caption reveals the direct relationship between the two apparently disparate scenes; this was a principle of construction Heartfield was sometimes to use in his later photomontages.

The first International Dada Fair, held in Berlin in 1920, included works by Arp, Picabia and Ernst as well as by the Berlin group. The highlight of the Fair, which led to prosecution for defaming the *Reichswehr* (German Army), was the stuffed dummy, dressed in a German officer's uniform with the head of a pig.[12]

The stated theme of the exhibition was 'Art is dead! Long live the machine art of Tatlin!'. The recurrent motif in the photomontages exhibited by Hausmann and Hannah Höch is the machine, yet their attitude to the machine is far from unambiguous. Beside *Dada Conquers*, which proclaimed the world victory of Dada, hung *Tatlin at Home*, demonstrating, apparently, the admiration and sympathy of the Berlin Dadaists for the new Production Art in Russia. However, Hausmann stated in 1967 that this was an accidental, haphazard accumulation of images, rather than a planned affirmation of 'machine art' – of whose manifestations, if any, in Russia, they had only the haziest idea.

25
26
27

27

Leafing through an American review, Hausmann had come across a photograph of a man which, for no particular reason, 'automatically' reminded him of Tatlin. He was, however, more 'interested in showing the image of a man who only had machines in his head'. From this point, images were added to balance and expand this first idea: the dummy with soft, organic insides, the man turning out empty pockets ('Tatlin can't have been rich'), the boat's stern with screw-propeller adding the final touch. As in *Dada Conquers*, the background is painted, a steeply receding, platform-like floor which, together with other details and a certain oneiric quality, is reminiscent of the paintings of De Chirico.

The photograph of Raoul Hausmann and Hannah Höch at the Dada Fair shows them standing in front of their photomontages, including Hausmann's *Festival Dada* (1920) in which a pressure gauge is mounted in place of a head. There are, clearly, parallels between photomontages and the constructed objects which include ready-made materials which became a prominent feature of Dada, and also heralded the Surrealist object. At the Berlin Dada Fair, besides the stuffed dummy in the German officer's uniform mentioned above, there was a dressmaker's

25 Raoul Hausmann and Hannah Höch at the International Dada Fair, Berlin, 1920

26 Raoul Hausmann *Dada Conquers* 1920

27 Raoul Hausmann *Tatlin at Home* 1920

dummy with an electric light bulb for the head, and a rusty knife and fork and military decoration attached. Such objects recall Huelsenbeck's comments on Zürich Dada collages (the 'new medium', as he called it) which he criticized for not taking the medium to its logical conclusion, by using 'real' things like a post office form.[13] Huelsenbeck was thinking here still in terms of the flat surface of the collage, but the step to the three-dimensional was inevitable and had precedents both in Picasso's Cubist constructions and relief-assemblages, and in Duchamp's readymades. The New York issues of Picabia's *391* (1917) had contained photographs of plain, mass-produced objects suggestively labelled, like the electric light bulb titled 'Américaine' ('American Girl'). Objects like the 'adorned' dummy or Hausmann's mechanical head *Spirit of Our Time* could be said to bear a similar relationship to the photomontages of Höch, Grosz or Hausmann as earlier Dada works, like Janco's *Construction 3* (1917), with its abstract exploration of the properties of wire, etc., do to abstract Dada collages.

28

In 'Dada riots, moves and dies in Berlin' (*Studio International*, April 1971) Hausmann mentions the influence of the Russian Jefim Golyschev, who made assemblages of unusual materials as well as collages. Hausmann's *Spirit of Our Time,* a wooden head with a wallet, tape measure, collapsible drinking cup and numbered card (among other things) added, was intended to express the petty bourgeois spirit of the times, unthinking, without individuality, reduced to a cipher and progressively dehumanized. Both the assembling of diverse objects to represent characteristics or attributes, to, in a sense, 'narrate', and the substituting of a part of the human form with another, often mechanical, object, are practices that have parallels in photomontage. *Spirit of Our Time* was, it seems, constructed after the Dada Fair; one of the objects that aroused considerable interest at the Dada Fair, and was reproduced on the cover of Huelsenbeck's *Dada Almanach* (1920) where it comes to resemble a photomontage, was an altered and partially painted white plaster replica of Beethoven's death mask, by Otto Schmalhausen, Dada-Oz, Grosz's brother-in-law.

29

Hannah Höch's photomontages, like *Cut with the Cake-Knife* (circa 1919), are often considerably larger than those of Hausmann, Grosz or Heartfield and are also radically different in composition. No attempt is made here to create an illusionistic space, as Hausmann and Grosz frequently do, nor the explosive fragmentation, the surface splintering of Heartfield's *Life and Activity in Universal City at 12.05 midday.* In *Cut*

14, 16–17, 31

14

30

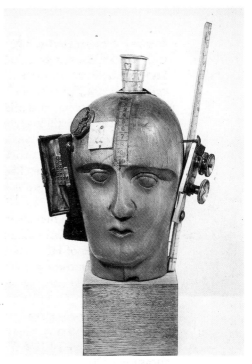

28 Raoul Hausmann *The Spirit of Our Time–Mechanical Head* 1919

29 Cover of *Dada Almanach* 1920

with the Cake-Knife, disparate elements, photographs and scraps of text are thickly scattered over the surface, but most still remain legible like words on a page. Yet where the paper is left blank, a dizzying and alarming space is created round the little figures suspended there. Cogs, wheels and other bits of machinery dominate the heads and bodies, which are often grotesquely re-assembled. The tiny head of a bearded man, for instance, tops the body of the huge baby on the right. Many are portraits of friends, fellow Dadas and the famous, and Lenin is seen beside Baader just above the inscription 'Die grosse dada' (The big dada), while Hausmann dangles, with the body of a mechanical puppet, just below. In the lower left section, several photographs of crowd scenes are pasted together, to construct an apparently more ordered but actually discontinuous space; the crowds are being harangued by a puppet-like demagogue: 'Tretet dada bei' (Join dada).

14, 21, 22, 39   Portraits and self-portraits are commonly included in the Dada photomontages. Hausmann, Grosz, Baader and Höch all included photographs of themselves or their friends, and sometimes the portrait

35 is fictional, as in Hausmann's *Tatlin at Home* or Baader's *The Author in his*

34 *Home.* In Grosz's and Heartfield's *Corrected Self-Portrait of Rousseau* (1920), the head of Rousseau himself is replaced with that of Hausmann.

30 George Grosz and John Heartfield *Life and Activity in Universal City at 12.05 midday* 1919

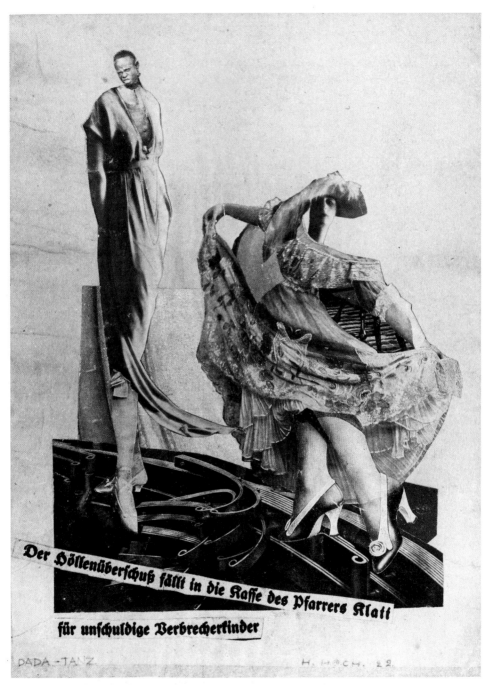

Der Höllenüberschuß fällt in die Kaffe des Pfarrers Klaff für unschuldige Verbrecherfinder

DADA-TANZ

H. HÖCH. 22

31 Hannah Höch *Dada-Dance* 1922

à mon cher
Tzara!
PRESIDENT.
BLO
OMFIELD.
HOL
LAND.
BLOOMFIELD
PRESIDENT DADA-
CHAPLINIST
BLOOMFIELD
PRESDENT
DADA
CHARLOTIN
Lydia
13

32 (*opposite*) Erwin Blumenfeld
(Bloomfield) *Bloomfield President Dada-
Chaplinist* 1921

33 Kurt Schwitters *Film* 1926

34 (*above, right*) George Grosz and John
Heartfield *Corrected Self-Portrait of Rousseau*
1920

35 (*right*) Johannes Baader *The Author in his
Home* 1920

14, 17, 27
141

33
135
The juxtaposition of the human and the mechanical was a recurrent theme in the montages of the Berlin Dadaists, and also in those of Ernst in Cologne and of Schwitters in Hanover. Although Schwitters emphasized the non-illustrational use of his collage materials, there are several works as early as 1919–20 which incorporate photographs, and he continued sporadically to mix photographs and engravings in his collages all his life.[14]

There was also a close connection between Dada photomontage and the Dada poetry of, for instance, Hans Arp, Tristan Tzara and Kurt Schwitters, which involved the random use of sentences from newspapers, scraps of conversation and clichés out of context, words wrenched from their normal associations.

In Dada collages and photomontages, fragments of text (usually from ready-made sources like their companion photos and engravings) are used in a far more aggressive way than in Cubism, in a mixture that often tries to deny the undeniable distinction between word and image. Texts are stressed for visual properties, and Hausmann on occasion used his own 'phonetic poem posters' as the basis for a photomontage, 36 as in *The Art Critic*.

39 *ABCD* (1923–4) is like a swan-song of Dada, a scrapbook of Dada activities. Hausmann himself, in a photograph that appears more than once in his photomontages, declaims one of his phonetic poems ('ABCD', the first letters of the alphabet standing for the sound poem), and has a wheel-like monocle drawn on his eye. Numbered tickets from the Kaiser's jubilee recall provocative interruptions of official ceremonies; the Merz ticket commemorates Hausmann's friendship with Schwitters; and the tiny scrap of map in the top right shows Harrar, the town in Ethiopia where Rimbaud, Hausmann's favourite poet, acknowledged by Dada and Surrealism in general, lived after renouncing poetry. What is the birth to which Hausmann refers with the obstetric examination cut from the pages of a medical textbook – Dada itself?

Hausmann was to remain loyal to Dada anarchism, but others, after Dada, took up more actively political positions. Looking back on Dada, Grosz and Herzfelde wrote in *Die Kunst ist in Gefahr* (1925): 'Our mistake was to have concerned ourselves with art at all. . . . We saw then the insane end-products of the prevailing social order, and burst out laughing. . . . We did not yet see that a system underlay this insanity.'[15] It was precisely this system that Heartfield was to reveal and make comprehensible, the better to fight it.

36 Raoul Hausmann *The Art Critic* 1919

37 George Grosz, cover of *Ma* June 1921.
Dada quickly spread to the numerous little
magazines that flourished during and after
the First World War. The Hungarian avant-
garde periodical *Ma,* which moved to
Vienna in 1920, opened its pages to Dada
from 1921. This was one of several
periodicals to marry International
Constructivism and Dada, whose mutual
influence in photomontage is of particular
interest

38 Heinz Hajek-Halke *The Banjo Player c.* 1930

39 Raoul Hausmann *ABCD* 1923–4

40 John Heartfield *The Spirit of Geneva* 27 November 1932

John Heartfield

Photomontage was used increasingly by all political factions in Europe and Russia in the decades before the Second World War. During the Spanish Civil War montage posters were made for both Franco and the Republicans; the Italian Fascists under Mussolini also used it extensively. But it is not surprising that photomontage is associated particularly with the political Left, because it is ideally suited to the expression of the Marxist dialectic. It was undoubtedly used most brilliantly by Heartfield, first against the Weimar Republic and then to chart the terrible rise of Fascism and the dictatorship of Hitler. In *Metamorphosis: Ebert, Hindenburg, Hitler*, Heartfield claims that the Weimar Republic was the caterpillar from which the Death's Head Moth/Hitler hatched.

41, 42, 63
55

60

Disillusioned by art school in Munich, Heartfield had worked for a film company in Berlin from 1916. After Dada, he turned more or less exclusively to photomontage, working for the German Communist press and designing covers and illustrations for books published by the

41, 42 Spanish Republican posters for distribution in France during the Spanish Civil War

43 John Heartfield, cover for Upton Sinclair's *After the Flood* 1925

43   Malik-Verlag, a publishing house which he and his brother had founded during the First World War. Hounded out of Germany in 1933, he continued to work from Prague, and then in 1938 took refuge in London. He died in 1968 in East Berlin.

In the essay 'John Heartfield et la beauté révolutionnaire' (1935) from his book *Les Collages,* Aragon describes the way Heartfield moved from chaotic Dada images to his unique kind of art: 'As he was playing with the fire of appearances, reality took fire around him . . . John Heartfield was no longer playing. The scraps of photographs that he formerly manoeuvred for the pleasure of stupefaction, under his fingers began to *signify*.'[16]

The contrast between the explosive, chaotic burst of Heartfield's
30   *Universal City* and the purposeful juxtapositions of the montage for
19   *Jedermann sein eigner Fussball* has already been discussed in the context of Dada. Few of Heartfield's photomontages subsequently retain the device of an obviously divided or fragmented surface, but the 1927 end-
44   papers for Dorfmann's *Im Land des Rekordzahlen* (*In the land of record profits*) do use the method of direct juxtaposition of separate fragments.

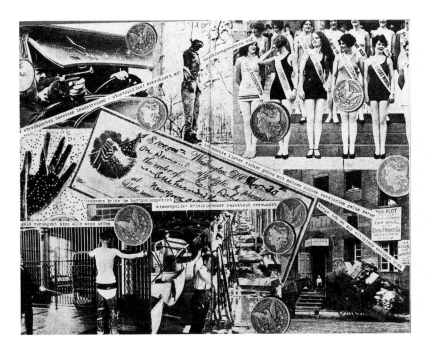

44 John Heartfield, endpapers for Dorfmann's *Im Land des Rekordzahlen* 1927

Here Heartfield contrasts images of beauty queens with a lynching, scatters dollars over the surface and intersperses phrases, perhaps from newspapers: 'strike pickets main roads – state police marches with machine guns'; 'I'd rather be safe with my hard-earned money – that's why I take it to the citizen's savings bank'; 'serious crisis in Minneapolis coal district: critical editor wounded'; 'money opens all doors'.

Heartfield continued to design book jackets and illustrations, often including photomontage, notably for Kurt Tucholsky's *Deutschland Deutschland uber alles* in 1929, but the great majority of his photomontages were published in newspapers and magazines: *Der Knuppel* (1923–7), the satirical weekly of the KPD (German Communist Party) which he co-edited with Grosz; *Die Rote Fahne*; and *AIZ* (*Arbeiter-Illustrieste Zeitung*) which was driven out of Germany in 1933 and subsequently edited from Prague. When his photomontages were exhibited, Heartfield always insisted on having copies of the papers on show beside the original, to underline the fact that his works were political propaganda aimed at a wide public, not private, unique, unrepeatable works of art.

49

45 John Heartfield *A Pan-German* 2 November 1933

46 Stuttgart police photograph of a 'peace-time murder victim' used in pl. 45

As images, Heartfield's photomontages are immediately clear and direct, however subtle the message may be. He used to save pictures from books, magazines, photographic agencies and newspapers, or have photographs made for him, and always called his works photomontages, even when using photographs unaltered or specially posed, on the basis of the caption. In the end, remarkably, whether montaged or not, they still *look* like newspaper photographs. The image fills up the whole page, and, however grotesque, remains curiously uncomposed, almost arbitrary; the immediate impression is almost that of an extraordinarily lucky piece of reporting. While the Dadaists, perhaps unconsciously, attempted to avoid the expression of an ideology – implicitly present in any image that is intended to represent reality – by breaking up images, Heartfield was able by juxtaposing them to reveal the ideology for exactly what it was, rendering visible the class structure of social relationships or laying bare the menace of Fascism.

In *The Finest Products of Capitalism* the unemployed man, with the 47 degrading placard hung round his neck as though he were an object for sale, stands squarely on the priceless lace veil of the bride, who is raised on a slight platform – altar, or part of the window-dressing? At first she looks like a dummy, but it is confrontation between two real people. The board reads 'Any work accepted': in February 1932, six million were unemployed in Germany. The German title *Spitzenprodukte des Kapitalismus* contains a pun on *Spitze*, which means both 'lace' and 'summit'. We hardly need the original caption, 'Wedding dress for 10,000 dollars, 20 million jobless', to see them also as symbols of the injustice of capitalism. They are both soiled by the inability of that system to treat anything as other than a financial counter.

In *A Pan-German*, a photograph of the Pan-German leader of the 45 brownshirts, Julius Streicher (who was editor of the *Stürmer*, an anti-Semitic newspaper), is placed over a photograph from the Stuttgart 46 police archives. This photograph had been reproduced in Franz Roh's *Photo-Eye* of 1929 as an example of photograph as document, with the caption 'murder in times of peace'. One version of the photomontage included the text 'The Womb is fruitful yet from which he crept', a quotation from Brecht's poem 'Der anacronistische Zug oder Freiheit und Democracy'. Streicher stands heedless of the blood under his feet, symbol of repressive authority, born of and nourished by violence.

The burning of the Reichstag in February 1933 and the subsequent trial at Leipzig – where the Bulgarian Dimitroff, one of the four accused

47 John Heartfield *The Finest Products of Capitalism* March 1932

48 John Heartfield *Hymn to the Forces of Yesterday: we pray to the might of the bomb* 12 April 1934

49 John Heartfield *The Sleeping Reichstag* 1929

Also sprach Dr. Goebbels: Laßt uns aufs neue Brände entfachen, auf daß die Verblendeten nicht erwachen!

50 John Heartfield *Goering the Executioner* 14 September 1933

51 John Heartfield *Through Light to Night* 19 May 1933

Communists, so successfully defended himself that they were all acquitted amid massive publicity, while the guilt was fixed (though without positive proof) on the Nazi Party – gave Heartfield the material for some of his most powerful photomontages. In *The Sleeping Reichstag* 49 Heartfield attacks the somnolent complacency of Parliament in the face of the rise of the Nazi Party. The Nazis themselves constantly and unwittingly supplied him with captions. For *Justica* 52 (30 November 1933) the text in *AIZ* read: 'The executioner and justice/ Goering at the Reichstag fire trial: "For me the law is a full blooded affair".' Similarly, the caption which accompanied *Through Light to Night* when it appeared in *AIZ* read 'Thus spake Dr. Goebbels: "Let us 51 start new fires so that those who are blinded shall not wake up".' A bonfire of books including the works of Freud, Kastner, Thomas Mann, Marx, Remarque and Tucholsky, representing the book-burning in Berlin and in various German universities on 10 May 1933, melts into and becomes a part of the flaming Reichstag. *Goering the* 50

47

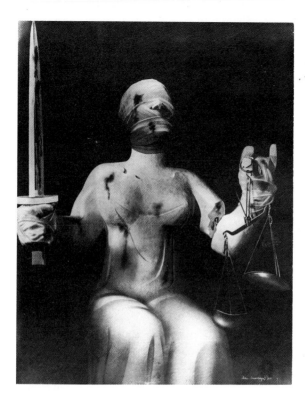

Executioner (14 September 1933) also refers to the Reichstag fire. Goering's face comes from an actual photograph and has not been retouched. The text reads: 'In Leipzig on 21 September four innocent men – victims of an atrocious judicial crime – will be put on trial together with the provocateur Lubbe. The real Reichstag fire-raiser, Goering, will not appear before the jury.'

The essential difference from caricature is that the artist has cut out and assembled real objects and events. As John Berger puts it in his brilliant essay 'The Political Uses of Photomontage': 'The peculiar advantage of photomontage lies in the fact that everything which has been cut out keeps its familiar photographic appearance. We are still looking first at *things* and only afterwards at symbols.'[17]

40   The photomontages which are photographs of specially constructed objects, like the bayoneted dove or the Christmas tree with its branches bent into a swastika in *O Little German Christmas Tree how bent your branches seem to be*, are an odd extension of this quality, because, although clearly symbolic, their effect is all the more powerful because

they are real objects. *The Spirit of Geneva* (27 November 1932) com- 40
bines a specially made object with photomontage. It was first published
in *AIZ* under this title, and was intended as a comment on the League of
Nations. The second version (1960) bore the title *Never Again!* and the
third (1967) had additional text: 'Peoples, may your children/all be
saved from war./Preventing war/shall be your triumph.'

Heartfield did not do his own photography, and W. Reissman, one of
the photographers he employed, gives a fascinating account of working
with him:

The photographs which I made for Heartfield, in accordance with an exact
pencil sketch and always under his personal supervision, often took hours,
many hours. He insisted upon nuances which I could no longer perceive. In the
darkroom he would stand by the enlarger until the prints were ready. I was
generally so tired that I could no longer stand or think . . . but he hurried home
with the photos still damp, dried them, cut them out, and assembled them
under a heavy sheet of glass. Then he would sleep for one or two hours, and at
eight in the morning he would be sitting with the retoucher. There he would
stay for two, three, four or five hours, always fearing that the retouching would
spoil it. Then the photomontage is finished, but there is not much relaxation:
new tasks, new ideas. He burrows in the photo-libraries for hours, looking for a
suitable photo of Hermann Müller, Hugenberg, Roehm, whoever is needed –
or at least for a suitable head, for the rest can be managed. Then he turns again to
the photographers, all of whom he hates, me included, because of the nuances
we are unable to perceive.[18]

In *Adolf the Superman* the montage is so skilful, the airbrush so 53
discreetly used, that the impression of a real figure, even down to the
unnaturally puny shoulders, is perfect, and all the more successfully
punctures the illusion of Hitler's rhetoric. The speeches that were so
essential a part of the Nazi programme are shown for what they really
were, not just bombastic but money-fed and representing the interests
of capital, not the people: he 'swallows gold and spouts junk'. This
montage was enlarged and posted up all over Berlin in August 1932
with the financial help of Count Kessler, the 'Red Count'. In April
Hitler had won 36.8 per cent of the presidential votes, and on 31 July the
Nazi Party won the largest number of seats in the Reichstag without
gaining an overall majority. The theme of rhetoric and gesture is con- 59
tinued in *Millions Stand Behind Me*, in which Heartfield renders Hitler's
salute ambiguous – from Nazi salute, intended to thrill and terrify
millions, it becomes a deceitfully open, grasping hand. An opposition is
set up between the apparent and the real significance of the salute,

which is de-mystified and deprived of its rhetorical power. The text
reads: 'The meaning of the Hitler salute: a little man asks for large gifts.'
55 By contrast, the poster made by Xanti for Mussolini in 1934 is simple
rhetoric, the visualization of a political commonplace: the leader at, or
as, the head of his people. But such is the capacity for photomontage to
suggest the opposite of what it intends, so narrow the dividing line
between thesis and antithesis, that I think it is possible, given an uncom-
mitted spectator, to see Mussolini as a lowering tyrant, devourer of his
56 people. There is a similar ambiguity in an anti-Nazi Olympics poster of
1936. It is Heartfield's genius almost never to let the significance of his
work be confounded in this way. The significance does not depend
upon the prejudice one way or the other of the spectator, with very
occasional exceptions as pointed out by Berger in his essay. He suggests
that the looming soldiers of the Red Army, towering over a tiny Hitler
54 in *The Suicide's Wish Fulfilment* (1935), are ambiguous, offering a threat
or liberation according to one's prejudice. He instances as a different
57 kind of failure the famous snarling tiger's head which warned against
the SPD, the Social Democratic Party. Heartfield and the German
Communists, Berger suggests, accepted an ideological direction from
Moscow condemning all social democrats, thereby losing all chance of
influencing or collaborating with the nine million SPD voters, which
might have blocked the Nazi advance. The additional text which
accompanied the picture when it appeared in *AIZ* reads: 'Social democracy does not desire the collapse of capitalism; it seeks only a way to heal
it (Fritz Tarnow, President of the Timber Workers' Union). The vets of
Leipzig [the Communist Party]: "We shall of course draw the tiger's
teeth, but first we must tend and strengthen him."' Though effective
superficially as propaganda, *The Crisis Party Convention of the SPD* is
weak in the kind of revealed internal evidence Heartfield's best photo-
58 montages contain. It also lacks the satirical force of, say, *Herr von Papen*.
Von Papen was the German Vice-Chancellor, who returned in October
1934 from a 'hunting trip' in Hungary, where he had held discussions
on the possibility of Hungary joining the Polish–German alliance. His
armband commemorates the purge on 30 June 1934 by Ernst Röhm and
the SA, in which von Papen narrowly escaped death. The irony is that
he himself, as Chancellor, in 1932, had lifted the ban on the paramilitary
Sturmabteilung in an effort to gain Nazi support in Parliament. The new
words to the old popular song suggest that he may yet 'leave his skin to
the bears'.

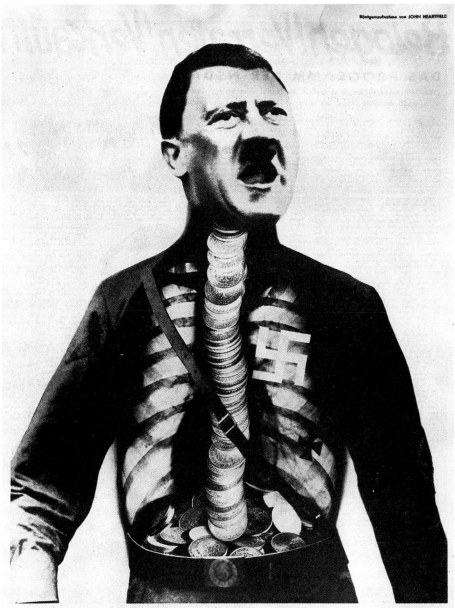

ADOLF, DER ÜBERMENSCH: **Schluckt Gold und redet Blech**

53 John Heartfield *Adolf the Superman Swallows Gold and Spouts Junk* 17 July 1932

„HINWEG MIT DIESEN DEGENERIERTEN UNTERMENSCHEN!"

54 (*opposite*) John Heartfield *The Suicide's Wish Fulfilment* 26 September 1935

55 (*above*) Xanti *Mussolini* 1934

56 (*above, right*) Dutch poster for the exhibition on 'The Olympic Games under Dictatorship' 1936

57 (*right*) John Heartfield *The Crisis Party Convention of the Social Democratic Party of Germany* 15 June 1931

Herr von Papen auf dem Jagdpfad

DER SINN DES HITLERGRUSSE

Motto
MILLIONEN
STEHEN
HINTER MIR!

Kleiner Mann bittet um große Ga

58 (*above, left*) John Heartfield *Herr von Papen on the Hunting Path* 11 October 1934

59 (*above*) John Heartfield *Millions Stand Behind Me* 16 October 1932

DEUTSCHE NATURGESCHICHTE

METAMORPHOSE

60 (*left*) In this *German Natural History: Metamorphosis,* as the original in *AIZ,* 16 August 1934, was captioned, John Heartfield suggests that the Weimar caterpillar Ebert finally hatched into the Death's Head Moth, Hitler

61 John Heartfield *WAR: Sudeten Germans, you'll be the first!* 13 September 1938

62 John Heartfield *Hurrah, the Butter is Finished!* 19 December 1935

63   Pamphlet issued by the Communist Party in Barcelona

As Lukàcs said, a good photomontage has the effect of a good joke. Many of Heartfield's best jokes – which in being funny lose none of their savagery – involve a literal translation of Nazi rhetoric. So, in *Hurrah, the Butter is Finished!* (19 December 1935), the text at the bottom gives a quotation from a speech by Goering: 'Goering (in his Hamburg speech): "Iron always makes a country strong, butter and lard only make people fat."' So Heartfield shows a family chewing obligingly on iron, while in the background photographs of Hitler are employed as decorative wallpaper.

Heartfield participated actively in the Spanish Republican government's struggle against the Franco-led rebels, and his influence is also seen in posters produced for them. In a pamphlet issued by the Comunist Party in Barcelona, however, the influence of El Lissitzky is more evident. This pamphlet listed eight conditions for winning the war, and

64 Montage for *Private Eye* March 1966

emphasized the need for strong governmental authority, conscription, discipline, unity, increased production and the co-ordination of indus- trial and agricultural production. Heartfield's own *Liberty Fights in Their Ranks* (after Delacroix) (19 August 1936, issued during the Span- ish Civil War) adds cuttings from press photographs of the defence of Republican-held Madrid to Delacroix's painting of the Paris barricades in 1830, *Liberty Guiding the People*.

109

Although Heartfield's influence has not been confined to the field of political photomontage, it is certainly strongest there. It is present in, for example, David King's anti-Thatcher poster, and in Peter Ken- nard's anti-nuclear posters, such as the photomontage using Con- stable's *Haywain*.

65
67, 68

The covers of the satirical magazine *Private Eye* usually combine text and photograph, and frequently use composite photographs which are not always recognizable as such. They are 'in the German tradition', as one of the artists involved says; but their political satire has targets like humbug, pretension and dishonesty, treated as local and comic, rather than revealing a political system.

64

Many examples of contemporary uses of photomontage could be cited. The Red Dragon Print Collective, for instance, produced a set of three posters in 1975 for RAP (Radical Alternatives to Prison) to protest against the setting up of control units in certain British prisons. In this one, the lower right-hand picture is reminiscent of Heartfield's photo- montage *I am a Cabbage . . .* in which a head is wrapped in newspaper.

66

58

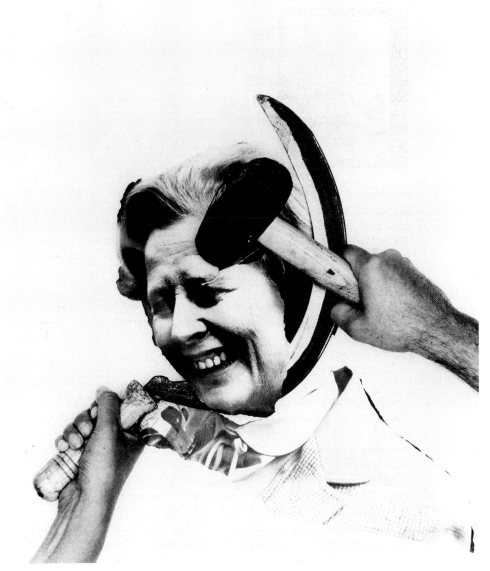

65 David King *A Short Sharp Shock* 1980

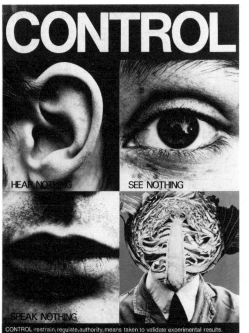

66 (*left*) Red Dragon Print Collective, one of a set of three posters (1975) for RAP (Radical Alternatives to Prison)

67 (*below*) Peter Kennard *Haywain with Cruise Missiles* 1980

68 (*opposite*) Peter Kennard *Defended to Death* 1982

69 El Lissitzky, poster for the Exhibition of Soviet Art, Zürich, 1929

The role of art in shaping and reorganizing, not reflecting, public consciousness was promoted very early in the Russian Revolution. Visual
propaganda was obviously a direct and successful way of achieving the
mammoth task of educating, informing and persuading the people, and
was particularly effective in a country whose population was neither
fully literate nor united by a single language. The agit-prop trains and
propaganda boats of 1919 and 1920, which went all over the country,
were covered with paintings – bold but predominantly traditional in
style – and slogans. Photomontage naturally took over part of this task;
as Lissitzky said, 'No kind of representation is as completely comprehensible to all people as photography.' Confidence in the accessibility
of photomontage in fact minimized the need for texts. It is interesting to
compare the agit-prop paintings with their direct descendants, the
street posters and the great montage friezes made for exhibitions, like 70, 71
Lissitzky's *The Task of the Press is the Education of the Masses* from the
Soviet section of the International Press Exhibition held in Cologne in
1928. While the posters rely on satire and opposition to make their
political point, the photographic friezes celebrate and exhort, showing
the great work of construction that is under way, the technological
advances and the growth of Russian industry – actual and visible progress witnessed through photographs.

Gustav Klutsis's statement 'Photomontage as a new kind of art of
agitation' was published in Moscow in 1931 and was also printed in the
catalogue of the photomontage exhibition in Berlin in the same year.
Klutsis emphasized the connections between photomontage and both
revolutionary politics and industrial and technological progress:
'Photomontage, as the newest method of plastic art, is closely linked to
the development of industrial culture and of forms of mass cultural
media. . . . There arises a need for an art whose force would be a
technique armed with apparatus and chemistry MEETING THE STANDARDS
OF SOCIALIST INDUSTRY. Photomontage has turned out to be such an
art.'[19] In his historical account of the development of the technique,
Klutsis claimed priority in the field of political photomontage. The
following passage from his statement was quoted by Hausmann in
Courrier Dada:

There are two general tendencies in the development of photomontage: one
comes from American publicity and is exploited by the Dadaists and

70 El Lissitzky and Sergey Senkin, photographic frieze *The Task of the Press is the Education of the Masses* for the International Press Exhibition, Cologne, 1928

Expressionists – the so-called photomontage of form; the second tendency, that of militant and political photomontage, was created on the soil of the Soviet Union. Photomontage appeared in the USSR under the banner of 'the left front of the arts' (*lef*) when non-objective art was already finished . . . photomontage in the USSR as a new method of art dates from 1919–20 . . .[20]

Hausmann quoted this to challenge the dates Klutsis gives, but does in fact seem to be overestimating the claim Klutsis is making, which was that the first photomontage in the USSR was done in 1919–20 (and names his own *Dynamic City*), and that agitational-political photomontage was developed in the Soviet Union. To support his claim to priority, Hausmann also says that Lissitzky, who left Moscow for Germany late in 1921, saw photomontages for the first time in Hausmann's studio. The question of priority between Dada and the Russian Constructivists seems far from being settled. Vasilii Rakitin states that Klutsis in fact first used photomontage in his design for a panel for the Fifth Congress of Soviets in Moscow in 1918, and that Alexei Gan experimented with it in the same year.[21] It would seem most likely that photomontage developed independently, among artists who knew about Cubist collage, although were not themselves practising it immediately prior to their first experiments with photomontage. And even if dating is settled one way or the other, the question of what was actually known remains. That El Lissitzky had not seen photomontage before doesn't mean Klutsis had not experimented with it though it does suggest that such experiments were not realized as public posters.

75

64

71 The entrance to the Soviet pavilion at the International Hygiene Exhibition, Dresden, 1930, with photographs and photomontages on the ceiling

72 Varvara Stepanova, illustration from the album *Gaust Tschaba* 1919

It is interesting that the international poster magazine *Das Plakat*, which succeeded in keeping its international character throughout the First World War and in establishing easy contacts with the Russians after the war, published examples of Dada montage in 1920, but there were no photomontages among the examples of contemporary Russian posters it published the same year: only the *lubok*-like and caricatured posters of designers like Lebedev. The essential point, I think, is that both in Berlin and among the Russian Constructivists there was an urgent need to move away from the limitations of abstraction without slipping back into antiquated illustrational or figurative modes. The photograph obviously has a special and privileged place in relation to reality, and is also susceptible of being manipulated to re-organize or dis-organize that reality. It is for this reason that it was in Russia, and in Berlin, where the impetus away from a predominantly aesthetic movement towards social concerns was most marked, that photomontage made its appearance.[22] A basically independent development is supported by the visual evidence, for in the cases of both Dadaists and Constructivists, the 'new' works using photomontage have more in common with the artists' own earlier works than with each other. The introduction of photographs in Klutsis's case is initially within the compositional structure of his immediately preceding Constructivist/Suprematist works. It was to alter his compositional framework, but never in the direction of Dada.

At the same time, the difference in character between Dada and Constructivist photomontage is evident, and the different circumstances in which each was produced were clearly to a large extent responsible. While the former, in so far as it was political, was satirical, and took as primary objects of attack the new Weimar Republic and German militarism, for Klutsis 'agitational-political' photomontage was visionary and utopian in nature, intended to persuade at first of the aims and later of the achievements of the Soviet state. The differences between Klutsis and Rodchenko are interesting here; Rodchenko's photomontages are more rooted in the everyday and can be ironic or humorous.[23]

Klutsis's *Dynamic City* (1919–20), which he claimed was the first photomontage in the USSR, is very close to and possibly preceded a painting of the same title and date, a painting on wood on which sand and concrete had been mixed; a lithograph of the painting, by Kulagina, also exists.[24] This planar abstraction, whose geometric structure is closely related to Suprematism, especially perhaps to El Lissitzky's 'proun' compositions (see p. 103), was exhibited at the Moscow Unovis exhibition of 1921.[25] In the photomontage, certain planes have been 'replaced' by photographic elements: a whole skyscraper (suggesting volume), and a fragment of skyscraper façade (suggesting plane). Photographs of workers engaged in construction, whereby other planes become steel girders, or a wall, are added, and the overall significance is clear – the Communist world of the future is under construction, a new world is being built (the circle = the globe). The introduction of photographs transforms what was in Suprematist terms a symbolic message couched in comparatively abstruse 'non-objective' terms, into a relatively accessible image. Klutsis added, possibly later, the following inscription to *Dynamic City*: 'Voluminally spatial Suprematism + photomontage. The overthrow of non-objectivity and the birth of photomontage as an independent art form.'[26] There is still, however, compared with the specific messages of later photomontages, which were often made for a particular campaign, more than a hint of the abstract visionary language of the founder of Unovis, Malevich, who welcomed the Revolution in cosmic terms: 'Innovators of the whole world, a new pole of the revolutionary axis is turning by the force of fire our heavy Sphere.'[27]

Both in this photomontage and in *Sport* (1922?), Klutsis favours a diagonal composition which enforces their dynamism. He suggested,

74
75

76

73 Gustav Klutsis *The Old World and The World being built anew* 1920

in one case, that the photomontage could be looked at any way up, and
certainly in *Dynamic City* there is no obvious 'right' way up, no fixed
point from which it should be seen, while in *Sport* the idea of rotation is
built in: the spinning of the trapeze underlined by the concentric
circles.[28] But *Dynamic City* was not designed as a poster, whereas by
contrast, certain photomontages of 1920 such as *The Old World and The*
World being built anew and *The Electrification of the Entire Country* probably were. The latter, certainly, was connected to Lenin's Electrification Plan, herald of his major modernization and industrialization
programme, and formulated thus by Lenin: 'Communism means
Soviet rule + Electrification.'[29] Bojko states that Klutsis planned to
incorporate this photomontage into a poster, but it was never realized.
Lenin strides into a circle (the world), which recalls Klutsis's earlier
geometric Suprematist compositions but is also now the base or centre
of forms clearly signifying building and also, in the bottom left, possibly radio transmission; he carries a pylon tipped with skyscrapers and
the title message. The radial dynamism of the earlier works is still
evident here, but less so in 'The old world and the new', where the
positive image of Lenin is superimposed over two circles in which the
old world, with its whips, chains and prison, is confronted by the new,
a circle framing Lenin's head and filled with construction work. In

73
77

68

74 (*above*) Gustav Klutsis *Dynamic City*
1919–21, photomontage

75 (*above, right*) Gustav Klutsis *Dynamic City* 1919–21, oil with sand and concrete on wood

76 Gustav Klutsis *Sport* 1922?

77 Gustav Klutsis *The Electrification of the Entire Country* 1920

78 Sergey Senkin, photomontage for a special edition of *Molodaya gwardya* 1924

1924, in memory of Lenin who had died that year, Klutsis and Senkin,
78, 79   with a contribution from Rodchenko, 'prepared a series of photomontages for a special publication. Today a rare museum piece, the work
contained fourteen full-page, two-colour compositions, most of which
were untitled. Hence it was called a "photo-slogan-montage".' This
was followed by a second photomontage publication, 'Lenin i dyeti',
also of 1924.

By this date, photomontage was established as a preferred Constructivist medium. Klutsis was certainly right in saying that photomontage
11   gathered momentum with *Lef* (Journal of the Left Front of the Arts,
1923–5), whose founders included Mayakovsky, Osip Brik, Tretyakov
82   and Rodchenko. The drive behind *Lef* was the need to link Constructivist theory with the practice of the individual artist, and to clarify the
position of art within a revolutionary society. It was an attempt to form
a broad front of artists on the 'left'. The editorial for the first issue of *Lef*
addressed artists as follows: 'In dictating orders to the factory from

79 Gustav Klutsis, photomontage for a special
edition of *Molodaya gwardya* 1924

80 El Lissitzky (studio) *The Lenin Podium* 1924

your studios you become simply customers. Your school is the factory
floor.' This echoes the demands of The First Working Group of Constructivists, set up in 1921, which had taken issue with those artists like
Gabo who held to the autonomous role of the artist, and dismissed as
'studio dreams' their belief in building up a new art to 'match' the new
society. As Rodchenko said, 'The same laws of economy and material
limitation should govern the production of a ship, a house, a poem, or a
pair of boots.' El Lissitzky, who attempted to bridge the gap between
these opposing groups, described the dialectical development through
which art had passed, reaching a positive stage in which 'art is becoming recognised for its inherent capacity to order, organise and activate
the consciousness through the inner charge of its emotional energy.'[30]

The fourth issue of *Lef* contained a statement entitled 'Photomontage' which stresses the special value of the photograph as document
and its appropriateness therefore for posters with educational and infor-
mational purposes.

71

By photomontage we mean the use of the photograph as an illustrative means. A combination of photos replaces a composition of graphic images. The sense of this substitution is that the photo is not a sketch of a visual fact, but an exact fixation of it. This exactness and documentariness give the photo a power of influence over the observer which a graphic image can never attain.

A poster about hunger with photos of starving people creates a much stronger impression than a placard with sketches of the same starving people.

An advertisement with a photo advertises the product more effectively than a drawing on the same subject.

. . . Up to now a qualified photo, i.e. an artistic one, has always tried to imitate painting and drawing, which is why its production has been weak, and has not revealed the possibilities there are in photography. Photographers supposed that the more like a picture the photo was, the more artistic and better it would be. In reality, however, the result has turned out quite the reverse: the more artistic it is, the worse it is. Photography has its own possibilities for montage and has nothing in common with the composition of pictures. These [possibilities] should be made clear.

As examples of photomontage in Russia, we can point out the works of Rodchenko in his book-covers, posters, advertisements and illustrations (Mayakovsky's *About This*).

88-95

In the West the works of Georges Grosse [*sic*] and other Dadaists are typical.[31]

117   The unsigned article was illustrated with one of Paul Citroën's *City/*
85   *Metropolis* photomontages; Popova's design for *The Earth in Turmoil*,

81 (*opposite, left*) Juryi Roshkov, photomontage for Mayakovsky's poem 'A temporary monument created by Mayakovsky to the workers of Kursk who first extracted the ore' (*c.*1925)

82 (*opposite, right*) Alexander Rodchenko *The Crisis* 1923

83 (*above*) Gustav Klutsis, poster for an anti-imperialist exhibition, 1931

84 Poster marking the fourteenth anniversary of the Russian Revolution, 1931

itself incorporating photomontage, was reproduced beside it, and the statement on photomontage was followed by Popova's notes on the production and set for Tretyakov's agit-prop adaptation of the play. A link is deliberately established between them. Not only does the design incorporate photomontage (for example, photo-portraits of the Czar and his generals are turned upside down and eliminated with a cross, symbolizing the passing of the old order), but the staging itself included cinema (projection of slogans and pictures), slides, special lighting effects and, it seems, actual objects such as a car, tractor and gun. The purpose of this treatment was to go for 'lifelike' as opposed to 'aesthetic activity', and to give 'the centre of attention to the agitational side of the play'.

Although Klutsis was right to say that non-objective art was finished by this time, much of its magnificent energy was absorbed into photo-montage. Most of the artists who were to use photomontage in an

85 Liubov Popova, design for *The Earth in Turmoil* 1923

agitational or promotional capacity – Rodchenko, the Stenbergs, Popova, Klutsis, El Lissitzky and so on – had previously worked as non-objective artists, and then between 1920 and 1922 explored Constructivist concepts in drawings and three-dimensional constructions with the impetus always towards the practical incorporation of their ideas into industry and technology. Although they resented the charge that, in their designs for textiles, posters, ceramics and so on, they were merely 'applying easel sketches to objects of factory production' (Brik), it is nonetheless true that the principles of shaping and 84, 86 organizing material developed during the early Constructivist days carry over into their later works. Klutsis's posters, like *Transport Achievement of the First Five-Year Plan* of 1929 and other works of the thirties, 87 retain the dynamic composition, with the emphasis so often on the diagonal, and the strikingly angled viewpoint characteristic of Constructivism. Lissitzky's poster for the Exhibition of Soviet Art, 69 Zürich, 1929, uses two heads photographed from his favourite angle – below the eye-level of the subject. The soft grey tone allows the two heads to merge as though looking into the future with a single shared vision, and contrasts strikingly with the sharp black and white of the lower part, which is either drawn or drawn over a photograph. Tension is set up between the abstract pattern created by the stark black-and-

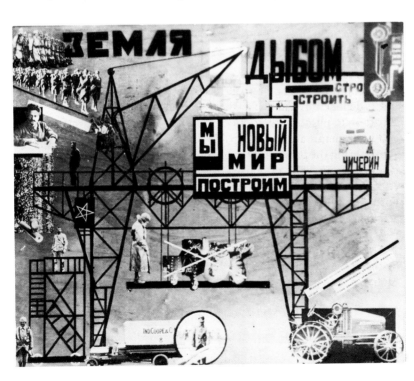

86 Gustav Klutsis *The Struggle for the Bolshevik Harvest is the struggle for Socialism* from the *Struggle for the Five-Year Plan* series of posters, 1931

white shapes and their existence as shadows and projections on the sharply receding façade of the building.

The emphasis on photomontage in posters, book jackets, advertisements, as illustration, the use of photography in wall friezes and on exhibition stands, must be understood against the gathering strength of representational easel painting. The 'First Discussional Exhibition of Associations of Active Revolutionary Art' held in Moscow in 1924 had included factions of progressive artists who favoured easel painting, a relatively naturalistic style and modern, heroic subject matter. Brik's text of 1924, in *Lef* 2, 'From pictures to textile prints', mounted a strong attack on these,[32] and 'Photomontage' with its stress on 'the combination of photos' as opposed to a 'composition of graphic images' should be seen in the context of *this* debate, not one centring on 'non-objective' art.

87 Gustav Klutsis *Transport Achievement of the First Five-Year Plan* 1929

In 1923 Rodchenko took charge of the layout and cover designs for *Lef*, in which he used photomontage, and made his first series of photo-montages to illustrate Mayakovsky's poem *About This*. They were among the first imaginative works in this medium in Russia, and bear witness to Rodchenko's assent to Mayakovsky's ideas. The core of the poem is a passionate demand for individual expression within a revolutionary society ('a redeemer of earthly love I'll be, alone') – if, indeed, they were still living in a revolutionary society, for Mayakovsky had fears ('our mode of living, which is now our deadliest enemy, making us petty bourgeois philistines').[33] The poem is on many levels an appeal against isolation – isolation from Lily Brik, his lover, as well as from society as a whole (Mayakovsky was regarded as a rogue Communist by practically everyone, including Lenin).

The photomontages, like the poem, move out from the particular, concentrated images of Lily to express the whole span of Mayakovsky's life and revolutionary Russia. His theme, Mayakovsky states, is love –

> This theme will come
> phone from the kitchen perhaps

– and the second photomontage shows him in his study, miraculously connected to Lily's phone across the whole width of Moscow. The next picture integrates two long passages from the poem – Moscow under snow, and Mayakovsky imagining himself becoming a polar bear (for jealousy turns a man into a bear):

> yesterday a man
> with one stroke alone
> of my fangs my looks I polar-beared . . .
> a white polar bear
> on my ice-float pillow I float by

Rearing up at the top of the picture he stands on a bridge over the Neva, seeing himself as he stood there seven years ago, and wonders why he did not commit suicide then:

> on its sky-scraper piers
> with aerial clamps it embroiders the sky
> steel soared from the water   a fairy scene
> Higher, higher I lift my eyes . . .
> There!
> There – on the bridge's parapet he leans . . .

88 Alexander Rodchenko, photomontage accompanying Mayakovsky's poem *About This* 1923

89–92 Alexander Rodchenko, photomontages accompanying Mayakovsky's poem *About This* 1923

93–5 Alexander Rodchenko, photomontages
accompanying Mayakovsky's poem *About
This* 1923

The following photomontage, from the second part of the poem ('Xmas 91 Eve, Fantastic Reality'), in its more static arrangement expresses the bourgeois home to which Mayakovsky turns, with its monstrous accoutrements. With horror he realizes that his host is himself:

> my very I
> Even Marx
> harnessed in a crimson frame
> A philistine load must tow just the same

The richness of the poem is obviously difficult to encompass in a single picture, but with counterpoint and juxtaposition Rodchenko creates marvellous equivalents. *Jazz* follows a series of images which starts 92 with a party and dancing heard jealously but contemptuously inside Lily's flat –

> dancing scraping floors
> . . . stamps into ears

– and moves on to La Rotonde in Paris: 'the walls in a two-step broke'.

In the next section of the poem, 'An Accidental Station', he has seen his own body from the air, then lands on the tower above the canyons of the Kremlin; in 'recapitulating the past' he makes a cross with his arms on the tower, is challenged by his enemies ('whole glove-shops flung at me') and appeals:

> I'm only poetry
> only the heart

But in 'The Last Death' he is killed in a duel with 'point-blank fire' (the cannon points up from the bottom of the photomontage), and the poet's tatters become the red flag on the Kremlin and the brother of the Great Bear.

The last two photomontages, from the third part of the poem, are quieter and simpler than the preceding ones. The first is retrospective, looking back on his childhood (the country child juxtaposed with the machines and radio tower of the modern city):

> in the very depths
> of childhood, maybe
> I'll find ten days
> fairly happy

The last looks into the future when, pleading to be resurrected,

96 El Lissitzky,
photomontage, 1931

97, 98 (*opposite*) Two
versions by
Rodchenko of a
standard cover design
for a series of detective
stories, 1924

95 Mayakovsky offers to do anything, however menial. He would even be
a keeper in a zoo ('do you still keep zoos?') and imagines he might meet
Lily again there ('for she loved animals'), smiling like the photo on his
desk.

This book is only one among several by Mayakovsky for which
Rodchenko made photomontages.

81, 99, 100 From about 1923 until well into the thirties, the uses of photomontage were rapidly extended in the fields of commercial publicity and
political propaganda, for posters, book covers, postcards, magazine
and book illustrations and exhibition installations. It was often combined with new typographic techniques to make simple, bold and striking designs. As Lissitzky said:

Most artists make montages, that is to say, with photographs and the inscriptions that belong to them they piece together whole pages which are then
photographically reproduced for printing. In this way there develops a

84

technique of simple effectiveness which appears to be very easy to operate and for that reason can easily develop into dull routine, but which in powerful hands turns out to be the most successful method of achieving visual poetry.[34]

Rodchenko devised a standard cover design for a series of detective stories in 1924, into which different photographic images could be slotted. The typography is incorporated into the design as a whole, which is governed by geometrical forms; the visual impact, here and in many other examples, is underlined with the use of abstract typographical elements, arrows, blocks, lines, often of contrasting black and red. The emphasis was on clarity, simplicity and legibility in the lettering, as in, for example, El Lissitzky's cover for Richard Neutra's *Amerika*, which also uses photographic superimposition. The use of plain, sans-serif alphabets was common to the Bauhaus, too, where Lissitzky had close contacts. His ideas influenced a number of artists and designers, such as the graphic designer Jan Tschichold. Solomon

97, 98

99

99 El Lissitzky, cover for
Richard Neutra's *Amerika* 1929

100 Solomon Telingater,
photomontage for Feinberg's
The Year 1914 1934

Telingater started work as a typographer in 1925; he designed books, posters and new type-faces, as well as making photomontages such as this one for Feinberg's *The Year 1914,* which reveals the influence of   100
Rodchenko.

Rodchenko's first work in industrial typography was the designing, from 1922 to 1924, of film titles for Vertov's 'Kino-Pravda', documentaries, or newsreel journals, covering the whole country. He 'approached these titles in a production spirit, treating them as part of the film itself, guided by its montage and scenario'.[35] This early experience of working with films must have influenced his photomontages, and, indeed, the dramatic development of Soviet cinema has close parallels with that of photomontage. The use in film of dynamic, rapid inter-cutting, disrupting unity of time and space and making comparisons and qualifications, the use of alternating close-up and distance   102, 103
shots, overlapping motifs, double exposures and split-screen projection, all have equivalents in photomontage. Hausmann described photomontage as 'static film'. Lissitzky's photographic montage for   70
the Press Exhibition, in its organization of material and its ideological structure, is similar to the documentary films of Vertov and others.

Montage in film, in the basic sense of editing, was of course internationally established practice, and Eisenstein had been experimenting with a 'montage of attractions' in the theatre – 'attractions' in the vaudeville sense, juxtaposing unrelated acts and events. The Russian film-maker Kuleshov, however, was one of the first to develop a *theory* of montage, and his ideas are interesting in relation to photomontage techniques. He explained how he started from the simple fact that 'every art form has two technological elements: material itself and the methods of organising that material'.[36] The methods of the cinema are very complex, but basically, Kuleshov assumes, its material is reality, and the structure given to it is all-important in determining how that reality is perceived: 'The interaction of separate montage segments, their position, and likewise their rhythmic duration, become the contents of the production and world view of the artist. The very same action, the very same event, set in different places with different comparisons, "works" differently ideologically.' Kuleshov himself used to synthesize details of quite disparate objects to create a sequence – once he created the presence of a woman in a film by combining different features from several different women.

101 El Lissitzky, cover
of the catalogue to the
Japanese Cinema
Exhibition, Moscow,
1929

102 (*below*) Sergei
Eisenstein, still from the
film *Strike* 1924

103 (*opposite, above*)
Dziga Vertov, still from
the film *Man with a
Movie Camera* 1928

104 Boris Prusakov *I Hurry to see the Khaz Push* 1927

105 Alexander Rodchenko,
poster for *Kino-Eye* directed
by Dziga Vertov, 1924

105 Rodchenko made his first film posters for Vertov's *Kino-Eye* (1923), 'a full-length "fact film" intended to demonstrate the latter's theories of documentary montage', for which Vertov, his brother and his cameraman travelled all over the country, 'visited markets with concealed cameras, rode with ambulances to accidents, spied on criminals from behind windows, haunted the doors of beer parlours, danced with rejoicing collective farmers . . .'[37] to get as close to a sense of real life as possible. In 1924 all film production in the USSR was centralized into a single organization, Goskino (after 1926, Sovkino). A separate department was set up for the production of film posters, called Reklam Film, and a stream of extraordinary posters followed, by artists like Prusakov

104 and the Stenberg brothers, Vladimir and Georgii. Prusakov's *I Hurry to see the Khaz Push* shows a man on a bicycle, his head and body made of clips from the film he is hastening to see. The Stenberg brothers made a

107 number of posters on agitational subjects, like *To the Fallow Ground* (1928), as well as film posters. They rarely used photography directly in their work, preferring to simulate the realism of photography. They worked from photographs, or from strips of film from film studios, and their work frequently resembles photomontage. One exception is

106 (*opposite*) Vladimir and Georgii Stenberg, poster for *The Eleventh* directed by Dziga Vertov, 1928

ОДИНАДЦЯТИЙ
ОДИНАДЦЯТИЙ
ОДИНАДЦЯТИЙ
ВИРОБНИЦТВО
2 СТЕНБЕРГ 2
АВТОР-КЕРЕВНИК ДЗИГА ВЕРТОВ ГОЛОВНИЙ ОПЕРАТОР КАУФМАН

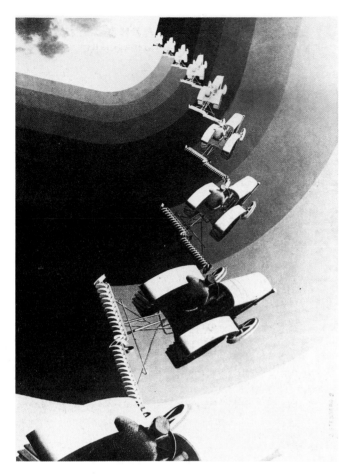

106   their poster for Vertov's *The Eleventh* (a reference to the eleventh
anniversary of the Revolution), in which the glasses 'reflect' images of
heavy industrial production.

In Poland, where Constructivism was also an energetic force in art
and design, there were interesting developments in photomontage.
The Polish Constructivists centred on the Blok group, which included
Wladislaw Strzeminski, Katerzyna Kobro, Szczuka, Teresa Zarnower
and Henryk Berlewi. In March 1924 the first issue of their magazine
Blok appeared, with a geometrical layout influenced by the trilingual
periodical *Veshch-Objet-Gegenstand,* edited by Lissitzky and Ehrenburg
and first published in 1922. Szczuka, who introduced photomontage in
Poland, abandoned abstract painting in favour of typographic design,

photomontage and architecture. He wrote, 'Photomontage brings about the mutual penetration of the most varied phenomena occurring in the universe . . . it brings an epic trend to modern art.' Closer to the productivist wing of the Constructivists than to artists like Gabo or Malevich, Szczuka's uncompromising position led to a split in *Blok*. His montage 'Kemal's Constructive Programme', reproduced in *Blok*, no. 5, 1924, celebrates the modernization programme of Kemal Ataturk in Turkey. It contrasts remnants of the classical past with symbols of the modern industrial world, in conception not unlike Klutsis's *Transport* poster celebrating railway construction, but lacking the dramatic contrast of the huge locomotive and the tiny camel-rider now rendered anachronistic by the engine about to crush him.

108, 87

93

DIE FREIHEIT KÄMPFT IN IHREN REIHEN

Nach Delacroix

112, 115

Mieczyslaw Berman, from about 1927, combined photographs with a bold Constructivist design in works that show the influence of Lissitzky and Klutsis, and are often dedicated to the achievements of modern technology. From about 1930, inspired by Heartfield, his photomontages become predominantly political and satirical.

109, 110

The use of photomontage in the USSR continued well into the thirties, notably in Lissitzky's contributions to the journal *USSR In Construction* (1930–41), an impressive and profusely illustrated quadrilingual publication reporting on progress in different areas of the USSR, produced collectively by artists, writers and photographers. Other artists, like Valentina Kulagina (who was married to Klutsis), worked on posters and exhibition designs; her poster for International Women's Day, or *Women Workers, Shock Workers, Strengthen Your Shock Brigades*, incorporates photographs and drawing.[38] Some worked in collectives, like the Brigade KGK, whose posters, like those of Klutsis, reveal Constructivist roots, and like him favour the juxtaposition of a crowd or group scene and an enlarged or isolated figure, or an isolated, symbolic gesture – a hand stretched out or gripping a flag-pole, for example. Klutsis, too, continued to make photomontages for posters (among other things) which still retain some of the dynamism, the

113
116
114

94

109 (*far left*) John Heartfield *Liberty Fights in their Ranks* (after Delacroix) 19 August 1936

110 (*left*) Mieczyslaw Berman *The Red Cap* (after Delacroix) 1969

111 (*right*) A. Sitomirski *Here's the Corporal who Generaled Germany into Catastrophe* 1941

sharply angled viewpoint, of the earlier Constructivist designs. Increasingly, though, the distinctive character of photomontage was submerged by the dominant pictorial heroic realism. Insofar as photomontage was a 'constructed' medium, with a non-organic character, it was condemned as Formalist. Although some artist-designers, like Klints and later Sitomirski, did follow the official line and took Heartfield, whose work was exhibited in Moscow in 1931, as model, photomontage never really revived after the Stalin era, and today, as Gassner argues, is little more than a marginal branch of caricature. It seems that a renewed taste for the decorative – a 'bourgeois' taste that Rodchenko had deplored and mocked in 1923 – contributed to its eclipse. This was the theme of a lecture for the opening of the Rodchenko exhibition held in Moscow in 1957:

111

Mention is often made of the asceticism of the artistic left wing. . . . This was an asceticism of simplicity, a straight-lined asceticism which brought an end to ornamentation. Our departure from asceticism has led to the proliferation of middle-class art on a large scale. When I gaze on the posters and covers of Rodchenko, they seem to be the beginning of something which was never continued. It is sad that middle-class art, as personified by thousands of pink lampshades glowing in the windows of new flats, has managed to nip these early germs in the bud.[39]

112 Mieczyslaw Berman *Construction 1* 1927

113 El Lissitzky, montage from *USSR in Construction*, no. 10, 1932, a quadrilingual journal reporting on progress in different areas of the USSR, produced collectively by artists, writers and photographers from 1930–41

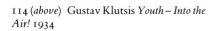

114 (*above*) Gustav Klutsis *Youth – Into the Air!* 1934

115 (*above right*) Mieczyslaw Berman *Lindbergh* 1927

116 Valentina Kulagina *Women Workers, Shock Workers, Strengthen Your Shock Brigades*, poster for *International Women's Day* 1930

117 Paul Citroën *Metropolis* 1923

CHAPTER THREE

Metropolis: The Vision of the Future

We will sing of great crowds excited by work, by pleasure and by riot; we will sing of the multicoloured, polyphonic tides of revolution in the modern capitals; we will sing of the vibrant nightly fervour of arsenals and shipyards blazing with violent electric moons; . . . and the sleek flight of planes whose propellers chatter in the wind like banners and seem to cheer like an enthusiastic crowd.[1]

Energetic and pulsating as they can be, Futurist paintings never fully matched the heroic vision of the modern world evoked by Marinetti in *The Manifesto of Futurism* (1909). The violent changes of scale and simultaneous perceptions of different things implicit in the vision of the Futurist city were, however, ideal matter for photomontage. The contrast between the surging masses in the city and its gigantic buildings, the sense of exhilaration in their very dominance, and the beginning of panic with the realization that the city with its buildings and machines can no longer be experienced as an extension of man, but is moving swiftly out of control and into a life of its own, are all expressed in the piled images of Citroën's *Metropolis* or Podsadecki's *Modern City: melting pot of life.* 117, 118 120

Paul Citroën made his first *City* montages in 1919, pasted together from cut-up photographs and postcards of houses, windows, staircases. He had been in contact with Berlin Dada, and from 1922 to 1925 was a student at the Weimar Bauhaus, where in 1923 he made his *Metropolis* series. There is an impression of dizzying space in these pictures, with the bird's-eye view of a street racing back into the distance in the centre, surrounded by steeply angled perspectives of buildings which stretch away as far as the eye can see. Citroën's work was perhaps an inspiration for Fritz Lang's film of the same title, a nightmare moral fable of a future society where only the rich live above ground. The skyscraper city in the film, with planes flying between the buildings, was a maquette with close similarities to Citroën's *Metropolis.* The montage of scenes from Walter Ruttmann's film *Berlin* (1927) suggests the clockwork rhythm of the city. One building looms up at 121, 122 119

99

118 Otto Umbehr *Perspective of the Street* 1926   119 Walter Ruttmann, publicity material for
the film *Berlin* 1927

such a sharp unnatural angle that it looks, ironically, more like a cathedral spire than an office block. By contrast with this work and with
Podsadecki's, Citroën's, in spite of its breathless obsessional quality, is
built up in ordered squares, so that there is almost a horizon line formed
by an even series of joins across the centre of the picture. Within this
vertical–horizontal grid, which anticipates Mondrian's *Broadway Boogie
Woogie*, each square acts like a window with its own vista; the effect is as
powerful as the more obviously dynamic diagonal construction of the
Podsadecki and the Ruttmann.

123   By contrast, a satirical photomontage by P. M. Bardi, *Panel of Horrors* (1931), was assembled for an exhibition of 'Rational Architecture',
and was intended to show the backward-looking, dusty attitude of
124   official Italian building policy. Similarly, Domela's *Berlin Museums*, a
panel made for the wall of the 1931 Berlin exhibition of photomontage
which he organized, shows Berlin's museums and galleries obsessed
with the art of the past.

100

122 Fritz Lang, still from the film *Metropolis* 1926

120 Kazimierz Podsadecki *Modern City: melting pot of life* 1928

121 Fritz Lang, montage of scenes from the film *Metropolis* 1926

123 P. M. Bardi *Panel of Horrors*
1931

124 César Domela-
Nieuwenhuis *Berlin Museums*
1931

125 Paul Citroën *Brotenfeld* 1928

The use of photomontage by architects in building plans and projections is now a commonplace. It has a practical use in, for example, showing the relationship between the existing environment and the projected building. In the twenties, however, it was sometimes used in a more personal way. Citroën's *Brotenfeld* is like a mock projection, 125 pointing up the unbridgeable gap between the country and buildings of the past, taken from an old engraving, and the city and buildings of the present and future. It is curiously hard now to judge the tone of the work – whether it was intended as a comic fantasy, or contains suggestions about appropriate building styles, or is simply a comment on the industrialization of the countryside.

Design and Construction of a House, Warsaw, the photomontage by the 128 Polish Constructivist architects Lachert and Szanajca, who taught at the Warsaw Institute of Technology and collaborated on several projects, combines plans and a view of the house – showing advanced construction methods for its time – with photographs of the two architects and of the house under construction, so that in spite of its utilitarian appearance it is more like a personal record.

Many of the great architectural projects conceived in Russia in the twenties remained unbuilt (as did in Italy the Futurist Sant'Elia's visionary cities), and perhaps the grandest of these was El Lissitzky's *Wolkenbügel* – this could be translated as 'sky hanger' or 'sky iron' – 127 which he demonstrated in a photomontage of 1925 erected in Nikitsky Square, Moscow. Lissitzky aimed to bridge the gap between the functional group of artists and architects and those who believed in the abstract search for an ideal form which would bring its influence to bear on functional work – as Malevich's *Architectonics*, a series of 'models' never intended to be built, were supposed to do. Lissitzky was concerned with the problems of suspending a building clear of the earth; as he wrote in *Russland*, in 1929, 'our idea for the future is to minimize the foundations that link to the earth'. Although probably planned to be built, the concept of the *Wolkenbügel* also leans on Lissitzky's non-objective 'prouns', volumetric constructions on canvas which he described as the 'interchange station between painting and architecture', and his 'proun-room', of whose space he wrote: 'We see that Suprematism has swept away from the plane the illusions of two-dimensional planimetric space, the illusions of three-dimensional perspective space, and has created the ultimate illusion of irrational space, with infinite extensibility into the background and foreground.[2] *Wolkenbügel*, however, which shows the building from the point of view of a man walking in the street, is startlingly realistic, making the visionary project *actual*.

189   In *The Non-Objective World*, Malevich demonstrated the sources of Suprematism with aerial photographs of dockyards, cities, roads, dams and aeroplanes in formation: the 'new environment of the artist'. His fascination with modern city- and industrial-scapes was conditioned by a new technology combined with photography that revealed a world unknown to earthbound man. Like his contemporaries, Malevich was
126   excited by the skyscraper city New York; in *Project for a Suprematist Skyscraper for New York City* (1926), he montaged a drawing of one of his Suprematist architectonics (forms conceived as pure, non-utilitarian architecture) on to an aerial view of New York, placing it, with a certain humour, vertically rather than, as it was intended to be placed, horizontally, thereby 'obtaining the highest and most modern of skyscrapers, that symbol of the Icarus myth pursued by his whole generation'.[3] Just to the right of the upright architectonic is the Equitable Building, for about five years after its construction in 1915 the largest and tallest of the New York skyscrapers. It is the building that can be seen in Grosz's
20   and Heartfield's *Dada-merika*, and also in Rodchenko's photomontage
94   for *Pro Eto (About This)*,[4] in which the poet stands on the Kremlin Tower, symbol of the old world against the new.

127 El Lissitzky *Wolkenbügel*

128 Bohdan Lachert and Joseph
Szanajca *Design and Construction of a
House, Warsaw* 1928

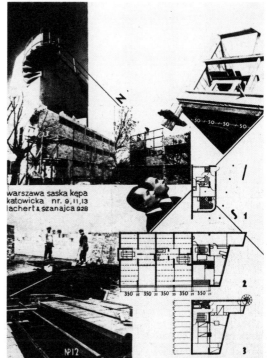

126 (*opposite*) Kazimir Malevich
*Project for a Suprematist Skyscraper
for New York City* 1926

CHAPTER FOUR

The Marvellous and the Commonplace

Just as the greater 'reality' of the photographic image as opposed to, for example, the drawn caricature informs political photomontage, so it can all the more successfully disrupt our perception of the normal world, and create marvellous images. By the juxtaposition of elements by nature strange to one another, hallucinatory landscapes are formed; commonplace objects become enigmatic when moved to a new environment. Our thought struggles to encompass them and is baffled, or a new thought is made for them. Different realities are thus revealed.

Before Dada and Surrealism began to pursue 'the systematic derangement of the senses', as Rimbaud called it, by pictorial as well as other means, the fascinating paradox of being able to distort reality with the medium which was its truest mirror had often been explored in illustrated magazines and above all in the medium of the popular postcard. These postcards, which proliferated after the turn of the century, used photomontage for a variety of effects: they might capitalize on the 3 disruption of scale, as in one example which showed a cart filled with giant Alice in Wonderland apples as big as its own wheels, with the caption 'Can a photo lie?'. Other postcards wistfully juxtapose an idea and a real scene – the young sailor embracing his girl rises from the 130 battleship on which he is serving – or manufacture by montage a tourist 131 joke: Piccadilly Circus is transformed into Venice.

The making of collages and photomontages was a widespread practice among the Dadaists by 1920. Some of Duchamp's altered readymades, like the colour lithograph of the *Mona Lisa* ornamented with moustache and beard, relate to this activity. Picabia reproduced a replica he made of Duchamp's *Mona Lisa* (*LHOOQ*), from which he forgot the beard, on the front page of his review *391* (no. 12, Paris, March 1920). Picabia's Christmas card to Arp and Ernst that year consisted of a pasted over photograph of himself, with inscriptions including 'Francis le Raté' (Francis the Failure). The title, *Tableau Rastadada*, refers to his 133 book of 1920, *Jesus-Christ Rastaquouère*, which contained nihilistic and mocking remarks about art. Both his photomontage and Théodore

129 Gyula Halasz Brassaï *Ciel Postiche* 1935, reproduced in *Minotaure*, no. 6, 1934/5

134   Fraenkel's *Artistique et sentimental* are concerned in part with fashion – high-heeled shoes in the Picabia, corsets and designs for aprons in the Fraenkel – a theme that is shared with many Berlin Dada photomon-
135   tages and with those of Kurt Schwitters.[1] Part mockery, part titillation, it is both a comment on taste and on the activity of shaping through cutting paper. Like the Berlin Dada photomontages, too, portraits and self-portraits are ubiquitous; there are, however, fewer references to machines, although these occasionally appear in Ernst's collages and were of course the dominant theme of Picabia's paintings.

In Czechoslovakia there was a group of writers and painters, including Toyen, Josef Šima, Karel Teige and Jindrich Štyrský, who were in close contact with Dada groups in Western Europe. In 1924 Teige founded a movement called Poetism which, under the influence of Apollinaire, favoured the 'picture poem'. In the summer of 1924, the group agreed to send 'tourist picture poems' from their travels, of which *Souvenir* may be an example. This group was to maintain a particularly close relationship with Surrealism in Paris.

131 Postcard of Piccadilly Circus as Venice, *c.* 1905

130 German popular postcard *c.* 1914

133 Francis Picabia *Tableau Rastadada*
1920

132 Louise Ernst-Strauss *Augustine Thomas and Otto Flake* 1920

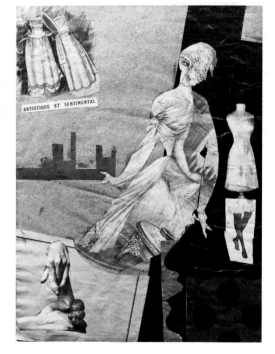

134 Théodore Fraenkel *Artistique et sentimental* 1921

135 Kurt Schwitters *Mz 158 The Kots Picture* 1920

Max Ernst was one of the first artists systematically to explore the 136-8 disorienting power of combined photographic images, and the possibilities of marvellous transformations of objects, bodies, landscapes and 140-2 even substance itself down to the tiniest detail. It was in Cologne after the end of the First World War, where, with Hans Arp and Johannes Baargeld, he fostered Dada activities, that Ernst began to make these Dada pictures which open up new areas of figuration.

As Aragon had noted in his essay of 1923 on Ernst, it was the free imagination working on and through given images that distinguished his collages from those of the Cubists. For Ernst, collage was the conquest of the irrational. This is how he described its discovery:

One rainy day in 1919, finding myself in a village on the Rhine, I was struck by the obsession which held under my gaze the pages of an illustrated catalogue showing objects designed for anthropologic, microscopic, psychologic, mineralogic and paleontologic demonstration. There I found brought together elements of figuration so remote that the sheer absurdity of that collection provoked a sudden intensification of the visionary faculties in me and brought forth an illusive succession of contradictory images, double, triple and multiple images, piling up on each other with the persistence and rapidity which are peculiar to love memories and visions of half sleep.[2]

The mechanism of collage did not necessarily for Ernst involve cutting and pasting. Once, when Ernst told a painter friend that he was working on collages ('glueings'), and was asked what kind of glue he used, he was 'obliged to confess that in most of my collages there wasn't any glue at all'. It was enough to add gouache, ink or pencil to effect a transformation on the page that resulted in a new coupling of realities. Frequently he intensified the poetic power of the collages with long inscriptions or titles. In *The Song of the Flesh*, for example, a handwrit- 137 ten text runs 'Le chien qui chie le chien bien coiffé malgré les difficultés du terrain causées par une neige abondante la femme à belle gorge la chanson de la chair'; it is a text with no logical or grammatical sequence and it reads like a collage of fragments. In those examples where there is actual collage, images drawn from photographic sources predominate, and Ernst often selected images of objects with a strong or interesting texture. He sometimes used x-ray photographs, as in *Here Everything is* 136 *Still Floating* (the title was chosen by Arp); a boat and a skeletal fish float together in the sky, a disorientation similar to that in the painting *Celebes Elephant*, where fish also are airborne and holes in the sky emit smoke. The boat is formed of an inverted and transparent beetle.

136 Max Ernst *Here Everything is Still Floating* 1920

137 Max Ernst *The Song of the Flesh* 1920

138 (*opposite*) Max Ernst *Health Through Sport* c. 1920

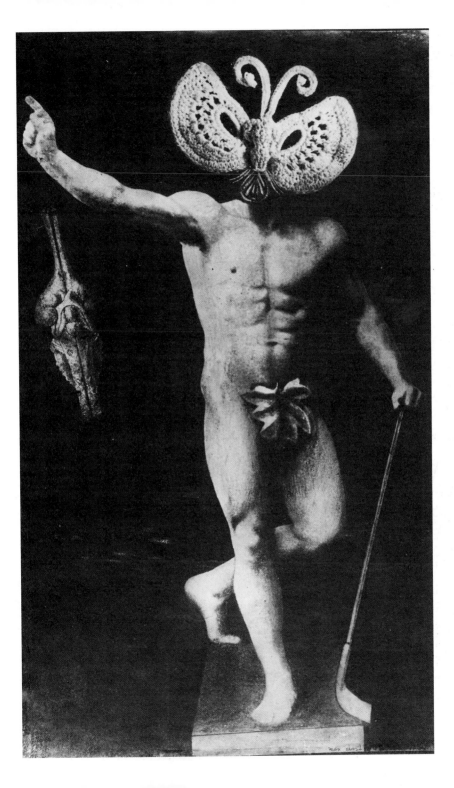

The special role of the photograph or photographic fragment is clearly recognized in these collages. As Breton said: 'He did not use materials aimed at an effect of compensation, as had been the practice hitherto (painted paper for painted canvas, snip of the scissors in place of the brush stroke, the glue itself to imitate smudges) but, on the contrary, elements endowed in their own right with a relatively independent existence – in the same sense that photography can evoke a unique image of a lamp, a bird or an arm.'[3] The isolation of an object can be as important as its incongruous juxtapositions: 'If one were to displace a hand by severing it from an arm, that hand becomes more wonderful as a hand.'

Ernst did not designate the different types of 'collage' by different names; he did not use the term 'photomontage', which at the time perhaps would have smacked too strongly of Berlin Dada, of which he had a low opinion, considering it a counterfeit version: 'C'est vraiment allemand. Les intellectuels allemands ne peuvent pas faire caca ni pipi sans des idéologies.' ('It's really German. German intellectuals can't shit or piss without ideologies.')[4]

Following contact with the Paris Dadaists Eluard and Breton, Ernst exhibited fifty-six of the 'collages' in Paris at the Galerie Sans Pareil in 1921 under the title 'La Mise sous Whisky-marin . . . au dela de la

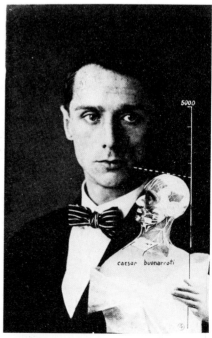

141 Max Ernst *Untitled* or *The Murderous Aeroplane* 1920

peinture' (Beyond Painting). Ernst also nicknamed them 'Fatagaga', standing for 'fabrication de tableaux garantis gazométrique'. Breton, future leader of the Surrealists, found in them an entirely original and exhilarating form of expression which corresponded with a quality he had been seeking in poetry. He saw in Ernst's work that surprising confrontation present in Lautréamont's image (so much admired by the Surrealists and providing the touchstone for their poetry): 'as beautiful as the chance encounter on a dissecting table of a sewing-machine and an umbrella.' As Breton put it in the preface to Ernst's 1921 exhibition:

It is the marvellous faculty of attaining two widely separate realities without departing from the realm of our experience, of bringing them together and drawing a spark from their contact; of gathering within reach of our senses abstract figures endowed with the same intensity, the same relief as other figures; and of disorienting us in our own memory by depriving us of a frame of reference – it is this faculty which for the present sustains Dada. Can such a gift not make the man whom it fills something better than a poet?[5]

In this preface, Breton recognized the dual role of photography, both in rendering obsolete traditional kinds of painting and in supplying the consequently lacking but indispensable element of figuration:

The invention of photography has dealt a mortal blow to the old modes of expression, in painting as in poetry, where automatic writing, which appeared at the end of the nineteenth century, is a true photography of thought. . . . Since a blind instrument now assured artists of achieving the aim they had set themselves up to that time, they now aspired, not without recklessness, to break with the imitation of appearances. . . . [But] a landscape into which nothing earthly enters is not within reach of our imagination . . .

115

139 *(far left)* André Breton *Automatic Writing,* self-portrait, 1938

140 *(left)* Max Ernst *The Punching Ball* or *Max Ernst and Caesar Buonarotti* 1920

There can be, in Ernst's collages, a balance between the comic and the marvellous, the axis on which much Dada and Surrealist photomontage turns. It is the transformation of materials, the juxtaposition that alters the nature of the original object photographed, that often provokes the disorientation that leads to what the Surrealists call the marvellous. In the *Chinese Nightingale*, where the head 'enfolds its thoughts like a fan, the head falling back on to its hair as on a lace pillow',[6] the effect is that of the Surrealist poetic image, the disparate elements meeting in an encounter that transforms them and, in this case, creates a new whole, a head like an ancient mask. When the effect is primarily comic, it is usually because the object stubbornly keeps its original nature (the hunk of beef in *The Song of the Flesh*, for instance), in spite of the metamorphoses effected around it and demanded of it, and the shock of contrast is that much greater.

142

Ernst's collages, though made under the sign of Dada, were among those works which heralded Surrealism, as both Breton's preface – in which he described them in terms very close to those he was to use in 1924 in the first *Surrealist Manifesto* to describe the Surrealist image (bringing two widely separate realities together and drawing a spark from their contact) – and Ernst's own later account from *Beyond Painting* reveal. Ernst saw these collages (as he also saw his *frottages*) as in a sense equivalent or parallel to Surrealist automatic writing, in that his 'visionary faculties' were provoked by the unconscious. However, during the first few years of Surrealism, the period covered by the review *La Révolution Surréaliste* (1924–9), comparatively few Surrealists persisted with photomontage, although the pages of the periodical were filled with *photographs*. Man Ray, of course, put photography to Surrealist use in a number of ways – in his 'rayograms', solarized photographs, double printing or double exposure, photographs of enigmatic objects – though he rarely used photomontage, with occasional exceptions like the later 'Self-Portrait' from *Minotaure*. As Breton said in *Surrealism and Painting*, while Ernst had been 'entrusting himself to photography's avowed aims and making use, after the event, of the common ground of representation that it proposed, Man Ray has applied himself vigorously to the task of stripping it of its positive nature, of forcing it to abandon its arrogant air and pretentious claims.'[7]

12

184

143

Among the photographs included in *La Révolution Surréaliste* were several by Atget of the streets and shop windows of Paris. Some, by the use of reflection but without any actual manipulation, disturb the sense

145

142 Max Ernst *The Chinese Nightingale* 1920

143 Man Ray, frontispiece
to *Minotaure*, no. 3–4,
December 1933

of reality of the photographic image. However, Surrealist art in the
twenties was on the whole dominated by a commitment to automatism
that tended towards the abstract, or towards the visible metamorphosis
of images. It was only at the end of the decade that, with the arrival in
the movement of Magritte and Salvador Dalí, there was a return to the
fixing of the 'dream image'. In 1929 Ernst published his collage novel
La Femme 100 Têtes, which used engravings, some of which are by
artists like Thiriat or Tilly who themselves worked from photographs.
Collages from engravings by Ernst were reproduced in the final issue of
La Révolution Surréaliste, as were paintings by Dalí and Magritte and,
144 significantly, three photomontages, one by the Belgian artist Albert
167 Valentin, the others by René Magritte. The Belgian review *Variétés*
paid particular attention to international photography and reproduced
works by, among others, Man Ray, Tabard and E. L. T. Mesens.
Mesens, who had been involved in both Dada and Surrealist activities in
Belgium throughout the twenties, poet as well as artist, began experimenting with collage in 1924, but subsequently abandoned it until
1954. In the twenties, he occasionally used photographic elements in-
146 cluding photograms (or rayograms) as in *The Disconcerting Light* (1926).

144 Albert Valentin, photomontage
reproduced in *Variétés* (1929–30)

145 Eugène Atget *Gentlemen's Fashions*

146 E. L. T. Mesens *The Disconcerting
Light* 1926

In 1931 the current Surrealist review, *Le Surréalisme au Service de la Révolution*, reproduced Max Ernst's narrative portrait of the Surrealist group, *Au Rendez-vous des Amis*, presumably to affirm the solidarity of the group. The title was borrowed from his painting of 1922 which had similarly celebrated the Paris Dada group Ernst had just joined. It is now more commonly called *Loplop Introduces Members of the Surrealist Group*; the head of Loplop, Ernst's alter ego, 'superior of the birds', appears above the internally framed group portrait, a picture within a picture. The individual photographs wind up snake-like from the bottom, with Breton as the fountain-head or root, rising from a lake, Man Ray to the right of him, Ernst himself in the centre, touched by the fingers of a pudgy hand, Dalí standing in front of him, with Tzara to the left of him, and a wind-blown Yves Tanguy at the top left.

The revived interest in photomontage among the Surrealists – an example by Breton was reproduced in *SASDLR* in 1933, entitled *Un temps de chien* (terrible weather, literally 'dog's weather') – can be related to the cultivation of the Surrealist object. This, like photomontage, worked with the coinage of everyday reality, because Surrealist objects were constructed from ready-made or found objects.

147

147 (*opposite*) Max Ernst *Loplop Introduces Members of the Surrealist Group* 1930

148 André Breton *The Serpent* 1932

149 Paul Nash *Swanage c.* 1936

150 Roger Leigh *Sarsens or Grey Wethers* 1974

In Paul Nash's photomontage *Swanage*, all but the lone swan buffeted at sea have been replaced by his own found objects, photographed separately but here combined to complicate and extend their individual and potent existences. As Nash said, 'The more the object is studied from the point of view of its animation, the more incalculable become its variations; the more subtle becomes the problem of assembling and associating different objects in order to create that true irrational poise which is the solution of the personal equation.'[8] Driftwood, stone and branch here loom out of Studland Bay on a gigantic scale. For Nash, there was an inherent Surrealism in both the found objects of this part of Dorset, worked on by weather and the sea, in the prolific fossil remains and above all in the Surrealist architecture and monuments of Swanage, which he described in his article 'Swanage or Seaside Surrealism'.[9] Sometimes, indeed, it is difficult in reproduction to tell the difference between a photomontage and a photograph of a composite object. In *The Torrents of Spring,* by the Belgian Surrealist Marcel Mariën, a tap sprouts tresses of black hair, and it takes a few seconds to decide that this is in fact a photographed object. In Mariën's *Crystal Blinkers*, one of the best of recent Surrealist publications, an enormous range of works using photographs, objects and sometimes words explore the metaphorical and subversive uses of photomontage. *Incest* is a fairly straightforward photomontage but in *Spirit of Laws* the effect of a montage is created by placing the symbol for 'and' between two breasts.

151 Marcel Mariën *The Torrents of Spring* 1966

Marcel Duchamp's cover of *View* (March 1945) is partly montage, partly fantastic and ingenious object. The label on the wine bottle is Duchamp's *livret militaire* (service record), the grey cellar-dust droppings of sawn grey cardboard. The smoke comes from a hidden pipe. The star-trek sky is a 'toothbrush offspring of frottage' (a toothbrush loaded with paint splattered on the paper). There were other stages in the montage involving 'magical little half-tone screens which push the peppery stars way back into the telescopic reality of the Milky Way, at the same time isolating and pointing up the wine bottle in all its glory.'[10]

The same issue of *View* (a special Duchamp number) reproduced a complex photographic montage by Kiesler, of Duchamp's studio and certain works, which folded in and out to create new contexts and combinations. Duchamp once used a family snapshop as readymade to be altered, blocking himself out with a black shape that parallels that which frames the entire image.

155

152 Marcel Mariën *Incest* 1968

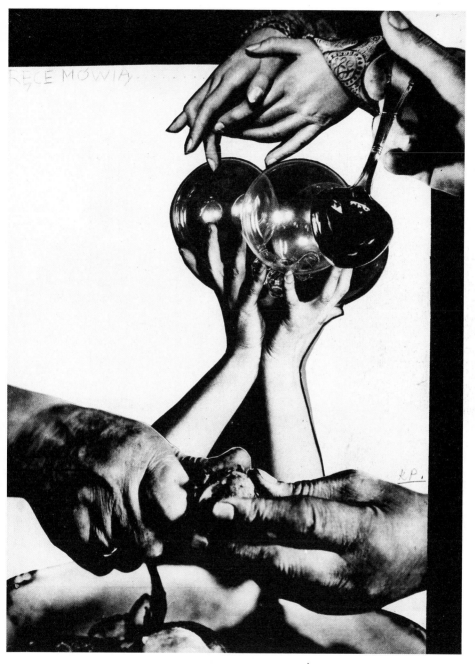

153 Kazimierz Podsadecki *Hands Speak* 1931

154 (*opposite*) Marcel Duchamp, cover of *View* March 1945

155 Friedrich Kiesler *Les larves d'imagie d'Henri Robert Marcel Duchamp* 1945, from *View* V, no. 1, March 1945 (Duchamp issue). The triptych shows three walls of Duchamp's studio on 14th Street, New York. When the cut-out panels on the flaps are folded in, the inner wall (and Duchamp himself) are transformed into a ghostly vision of his Large Glass, *The Bride Stripped Bare by her Bachelors, Even*

156 Marcel Duchamp *Family Portrait, 1899* 1964

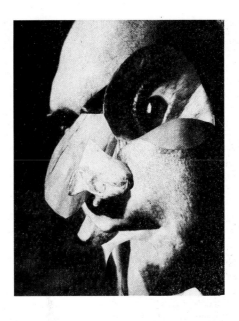

158 Raoul Hausmann,
photomontage, 1947

In the early thirties, special stress was laid on the 'symbolic function-
ing', in an erotic sense, of the Surrealist object. While the early Surrealist objects might function analogically, or invoke fetishism,
photomontage could work in an apparently more direct way on the   157-9
human body. Ernst, Baargeld and Höch, for instance, already in their   160, 162
Dada photomontages, disrupt, truncate or replace parts of the body,   16
rendering the familiar strange. The body can be re-conjugated as oddly
and troublingly as are Bellmer's Surrealist dolls, with disrupted scale,   161
replacement or repetition. The practice of doubling is one that becomes
central to Surrealist photography. Doubling, of course, is not restricted
to photomontage, nor to Surrealism. Florence Henri, who would   168
normally be associated with the Bauhaus and with non-objective
photography, used mirrors and framing devices to achieve a similar
effect. Man Ray's doubled breasts (from *La Révolution Surréaliste*) and
Brassaï's *Ciel Postiche*, reproduced in *Minotaure*, no. 6, 1934/5, use this
device in different ways. Brassaï constructs, from the montage of two   129
parts of a torso, a lowering hilly landscape. It appears to be a folding, a
kind of inverted repetition, of the same image but is in fact the juxtaposition of the front and back views of the body. The horizontal
alignment of the nude in Brassaï's photomontage is 'natural' but often
the cut-out part of the body or object is rotated to de-familiarize it
further.

157 Hannah Höch *From an Ethnographic
Museum* 1929

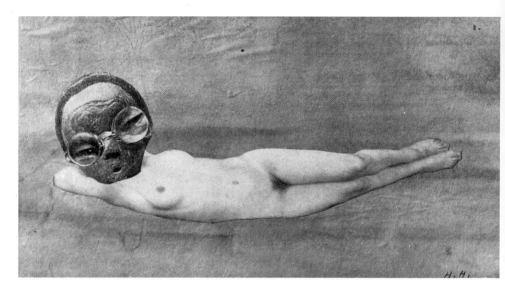

159 Hannah Höch *Foreign Beauty* 1929

160 Max Ernst *Les Pléiades* 1921

161 Pierre Molinier
Les Hanel 2 1928

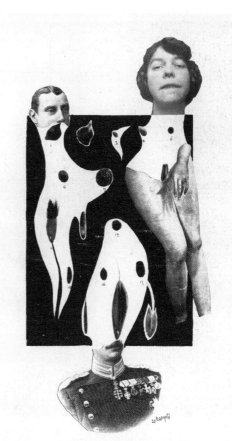

162 Johannes Baargeld
*Venus and the Game of
the Kings* 1920

163 Frederick Sommer *Max Ernst* 1946

Raoul Ubac, a number of whose works were reproduced in *Minotaure* (1933–9), developed various techniques by which objects, the body, the landscape or city-scape were subjected to a process of transformation. He used, like Man Ray, solarization and also petrification, by which the image is sandwich-printed slightly out of register, which gives the effect of a shallow relief. *The Wall* and *Penthesilia* (both 1937) were produced by a complex process of montage and petrification.

While photographers experimented with new techniques – besides Man Ray and Ubac, one could add in connection with Surrealism Dora Maar, David Hare, Frederick Sommer – for the artists, writers and poets of the movement photomontage and collage were, like the Surrealist object, accessible as an activity. The craft skills of the painter were not necessary. Breton himself, the poet Paul Eluard and his wife Nusch were among those who produced collages and photomontages.

164

163

139, 148

132

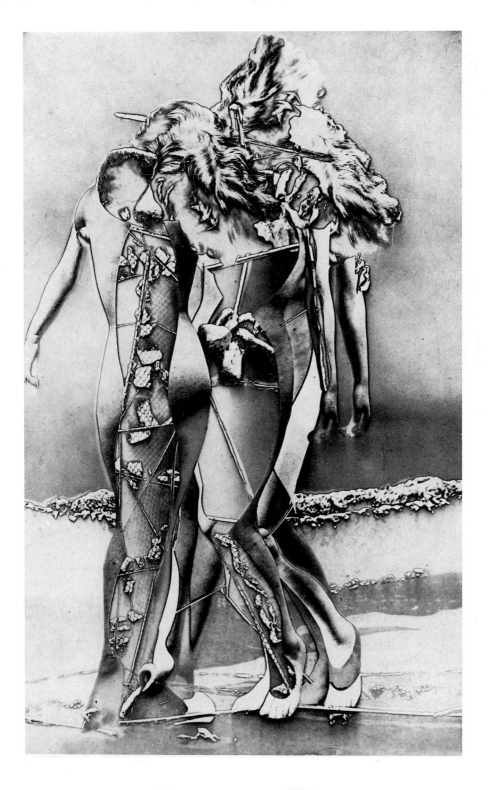

165 Georges Hugnet *Untitled* 1936

166 Joseph Cornell *Untitled* (Breton collage) 1966

Joseph Cornell, one of the first Americans to be influenced by Surrealism and best known for his fantastic object-boxes, turned increasingly to the making of collages using primarily photographic reproduction; for example, he combined a solarized portrait of Breton by Man Ray with the cut-out photograph of a faceted rock crystal. Georges Hugnet, poet and bookbinder, constructed a number of collages and objects.

By the thirties, what had become known as a 'Surrealist' mode was well established in commercial and fashion photography. This might involve montage, or the massing of bizarre objects around the figure or in the scene that was to be photographed. Cecil Beaton and Angus McBean, for example, employ what they clearly think of as a Surrealist mode. The equation they make is between 'Surrealist' and 'fantastic', and so embedded has this equation become that even Susan Sontag can write, 'The Surrealist legacy for photography came to seem trivial as the Surrealist repertoire of fantasies and props was rapidly absorbed into high fashion in the 1930s . . .'[11] The point that should be made is that the manipulated or theatricalized photograph is actually in a minority in the Surrealist reviews, and the greatest Surrealist montages, like Brassaï's *Ciel Postiche*, while admittedly manipulated, are so in such a way that the process is at first hidden. This montage reveals a further reality, not a substitution of a fantastic for a real world. It bears out precisely what Sontag, again, says: 'Surrealism lies at the heart of the photographic enterprise: in the very creation of a duplicate world, of a

166

165

129

167 René Magritte *Paris Opera* 1929

reality in the second degree . . .' The manipulation serves in this case to
emphasize and illuminate the duplication. The problem arises because
of a narrow understanding of Surrealism. It has come to stand for a
suppression of the real, a substitution of the fantastic for a 'discredited'
world of reality, whereas what it was concerned with was an extension
and deepening of what is understood by 'the real'.[12]

It is noticeable that the abrupt disruptions of scale that were a common feature of Dada photomontages (with Ernst and Höch, for instance) are less common in Surrealism, or at least less obvious as such.
Disjunctions and dislocations occur within the 'real' scene, as in Magritte's *Opera*, which rises in the middle of a field of cows. Unlike the
fragmentation of the Dada collage or photomontage, there is an apparent continuity of space. When, as must be the case in the metaphorical
treatment of body/landscape, there is an alteration of scale as in Brassaï's *Ciel Postiche*, this 'alteration' is not immediately made visible.

Games with scale are often central to the recent photomontages by Hans Hollein (which do have parallels with Ernst's Dada

31, 32, 14

170, 181
167

136

168 Florence Henri *Abstract Composition* 1932

photomontages); an object or part of an object is isolated and placed in a landscape which is strange to it, but with which unexpected analogies are set up: a Rolls Royce radiator grill rises up among the Manhattan skyscrapers, incongruously paralleling their shapes.

Superimposition can make objects or parts of the body which are of a different scale apparently exist on the same spatial plane, as in Slinger's *The Abysmal*; Tabard, who often used superimposition, achieves a similar effect in *Hand and Woman* (1929). 176 172

Herbert Bayer, though not a Surrealist and who in fact taught at the Bauhaus and was best known for his graphic design and typographic innovations, practised the witty manipulation of photographs in a manner which clearly has the 'Surrealist dream' in mind. In *The Language of Letters*, the woman's body is constructed of the sky. It obviously has something in common with Magritte but perhaps lacks the ontological dimensions of Magritte's transformations, where it is, for instance, a *bird* that is made of sky. In the thirties, Bayer made photomontages for the covers of *Die Neue Linie*. 169 171

137

169 Herbert Bayer *The Language of Letters* 1931

170 Jerry Uelsmann *Untitled* 1984

171 Herbert Bayer *Lonely Metropolitan* 1932

172 Maurice Tabard *Hand and Woman* 1929

173 Eduardo Paolozzi *Collage over African Sculpture* 1960

The practice of photomontage continued during and after the war with a new generation of Surrealist artists, and also with artists who did not necessarily owe any particular allegiance to the movement. The 170, 177 most interesting include Barbara Morgan, Jerry Uelsmann and, in a less straightforward relationship to Surrealist photomontage, the Catalan 175, 178 artist Jordi Cerdà. Jacques Brunius, who was a writer and film–maker, 146 left France for England in 1940 where, together with E. L. T. Mesens, he helped spread Surrealist ideas (*Ad nauseum,* 1944). Conroy Maddox joined the English Surrealist group in 1944 after working in Paris. Although he uses mainly oil and gouache, he has also made a number of 179 particularly humorous montages.

Collage and montage of photographs (not on the whole in the dark-room) are among the staples of the post-war Pop artists, like Paolozzi and Richard Hamilton. Paolozzi's works frequently comment on the proliferation of visual material available to the artist – scientific, tech-nological, art-historical, ethnographic – to suggest that our culture 173 itself is a kind of ethnographic collage (*Collage over African Sculpture,*

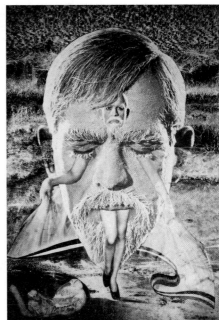

174 Nigel Henderson *Head of a Man* 1956   175 Jacques Brunius *Ad nauseam* 1944

1960). Richard Hamilton goes to great lengths to ensure realistic space in his inventory of indispensable objects for the modern home, *Just what is it that makes today's homes so different, so appealing?*, a collage of cuttings from magazines which was made for the poster and catalogue of the exhibition 'This Is Tomorrow'. Some of the photographic fragments are transformed, but in a deadpan way, so that the patterned carpet is a crowded beach scene and the ceiling an early satellite view of earth. The indispensable categories for tomorrow's world were, for Hamilton: 'Woman Food History Newspapers Cinema Domestic appliances Cars Space Comics TV Telephone Information'. These are strung together without irony like the apparently straightforward assemblage of photographic images, which are without emphatic changes of scale. 182

It is in the field of advertising, perhaps, that photomontage has become most familiar today – in the creation of the strange and marvellous, in the sense of magic and images and in the rendering enigmatic of isolated commonplace images.

176 Penny Slinger *The Abysmal* 1975

178 Jordi Cerdà *Suite Freud-Lacon* 1983

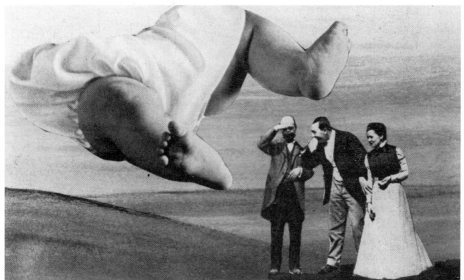

179 Conroy Maddox *Uncertainty of the Day* 1940

177 *(left)* Jerry Uelsmann *Untitled* 1983

180 Lajos Kassak *The Raven* 1924

182 Richard Hamilton *Just what is it that makes today's homes so different, so appealing?*

181 (*left*) Terry Gilliam, montage for the
BBC television series *Monty Python's Flying
Circus* 1971

183 Laszlo Moholy-Nagy *Structure of the World* 1927

CHAPTER FIVE

Photomontage and Non-Objective Art

The relationship between photomontage and non-objective art is perhaps not an obvious one, but it is nonetheless reciprocal and full of productive tension. The structure of certain photomontages, for example those of the Russian and Polish Constructivists, was naturally dependent on the principles of constructive, non-objective design. Conversely, the camera and photographic processes in general were found to be capable of suggesting forms, patterns and textures independent of the visible world and rich in possibilities.

Man Ray's 'rayograms' (in which objects are exposed directly onto 184 photo-sensitive paper), in stripping the object of its normal context, often also thereby strip it of its identity, so that new and independent forms are, apparently, created.

Herbert Bayer's photomontage *Metamorphosis* wittily suggests a 187 strange relationship between non-objective and representational forms. He has taken the basic geometrical shapes that he used in his design for the cover of the first issue of the *Bauhaus* periodical in 1928 (made while 186 he was building up the graphic design workshop at the Dessau Bauhaus), and shows them tumbling out of a dark cave towards a romantic landscape. Perhaps Bayer is also gently satirizing here the Platonic assumptions of non-objective art, with its use of basic 'ideal' forms, by placing them in the mouth of a cave so that they become, as it were, Plato's ideal objects of which we, mankind, living in the dark, facing away from the light, see only the shadows on the wall.

El Lissitzky's superb and famous self-portrait, *The Constructor*, was 188 made by a combination of superimposed negatives and direct exposure. He has literally integrated the artist's eye and his hand holding a pair of compasses with the circle and rectangles on graph paper showing the alphabet of forms, the abstract basis of Constructivist art.

Klutsis and Kassak, among others, based their photomontages on a 180 dynamic, abstract framework. Klutsis's *Sport* is close to his work in 76 other mediums such as painting and drawing, and is based on the composition in *Dynamic City*, which was inspired by Malevich's 74

147

Suprematism and Lissitzky's 'prouns'. In his photomontages, figures
or buildings are substituted for or added to the planes and volumes of
the abstract works. It is interesting that the origins of Suprematism,
which expressed the 'new environment of the artist', were demon-
189 strated by Malevich in a montage of photographs of bird's-eye views of
cities, docks, roads and dams.

Photography for Moholy-Nagy was of inestimable value in educating the eye to what he called the 'new vision'. He believed that in our
efforts to come to terms with the age of technology, to become part of it
and not to sink back into a retrogressive symbolism or expressionism,
the camera with its capacity 'to complete or supplement our optical
instrument, the eye' would help us to disengage ourselves from traditional perceptual habits. Moholy's ideas have perhaps been more in-
fluential than his works in any of the mediums in which he experimented; but probably his most original and exciting compositions
are those using photographs or photographic processes. His 'photo-
185 grams', as he called them, are more distanced from the world of objects

148

184 (*far left*) Man Ray *Rayogram: Kiki Drinking* 1922

185 (*left*) Laszlo Moholy-Nagy *Photogram: Lightening Rod* 1940

186 (*right*) Herbert Bayer, cover of *Bauhaus 1* 1928

187 Herbert Bayer *Metamorphosis* 1936

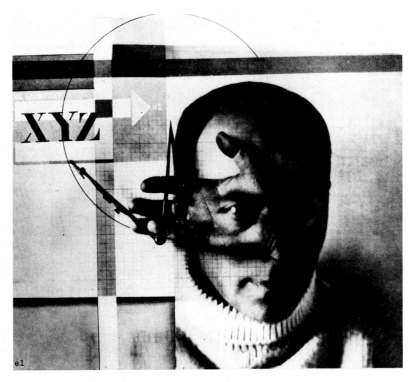

188 El Lissitzky *The Constructor*, self-portrait, 1924

184, 191 from fantasy creations, than Man Ray's, and are closer perhaps to those of Christian Schad. The direct records of forms on light-sensitive paper were particularly fascinating for him, being almost pure experiments in light and shadow, produced with the minimum of handling, and with the bonus of surprise in the result. In a letter to Beaumont Newhall in 1937 he wrote: 'I would think that photogram is a better name than "shadowgraph" because – at least in my experiments – I used or tried to use not alone shadows of solid transparent and translucent objects but really light effects themselves e.g. lenses, liquids, crystals and so on.'[1]

Moholy's photomontages, or 'photoplastics' as he sometimes preferred to call them when photographs were combined with drawing, are very varied: he was fully aware of the vast range of possibilities in the field. This is how he described his photomontages in *Painting Photography Film*: 'They are pieced together from various photographs and are an experimental method of simultaneous representation; compressed interpenetration of visual and verbal wit; weird combinations

KUBISMUS FUTURISMUS SUPREMATISMUS

189 Kazimir Malevich *Analytical Chart c.* 1925

of the most realistic, imitative means which pass into imaginary spheres. They can, however, also be forthright, tell a story; more veristic "than life itself".[2] And he added: 'It will soon be possible to do this work, at present still in its infancy and done by hand, mechanically, with the aid of projections and new printing processes.' But it is not surprising, given his whole-hearted and optimistic, though not dogmatic, commitment to non-objective art, that he should reveal new relationships between photomontage and non–objective construction. In the marvellously clear image of *Leda and the Swan*, while there is an interest in the subject-matter ('the myth inverted', as Moholy said), the main interest is in the spatial possibilities of the medium. As he wrote in 'Space, Time and the Photographer': 'Linear elements, structural pattern, close-up, and isolated figures are here the elements for a space articulation. Pasted on a white surface these elements seem to be embedded in infinite space, with clear articulation of nearness and distance. The best description of their effect would be to say that each

190

151

190 Laszlo Moholy-Nagy *Leda and the Swan* 1925

191 Christian Schad *Schadograph* 1918

element is pasted on vertical glass planes, which are set up in an endless series each behind the other.'[3]

The idea of a photographic sequence or series, which was the basis of some of Moholy's most striking photomontages, had a particular relation to the qualities of mechanical reproduction of the photograph: 'repetition as a space–time organizational motif, which, in such wealth and exactitude, could be achieved only by means of the technical, industrialized system of reproduction characteristic of our time'. The repetition of an image, Moholy believed, minimized its particularity as a representation, and enabled it to become a unit, a part of an overall design: 'The series is no longer a "picture", and none of the canons of pictorial aesthetics can be applied to it. Here the separate picture loses its identity as such and becomes a detail of assembly, an essential structural element of the whole which is the thing itself. In this concatenation of its separate but inseparable parts a photographic series inspired by a definite purpose can become at once the most potent weapon and the tenderest lyric.'[4] Delicately, in *The Law of Series*, and with more vivid 192

153

192 Laszlo Moholy-Nagy *The Law of Series* 1925

193 Jan Tschichold, film poster, 1928

195   fantasy in *The Shooting Gallery*, Moholy repeats an image, but with such variations that a counterpoint is created between its identity as a structural element and its identity as a picture. Andy Warhol, in his paintings and screen prints on canvas of Coca-Cola bottles or soup tins, repeats the same image until it becomes a decorative overall design.

    The subtle differences of exposure in each repeated image of *The Law of Series* are significant in building up an abstract pattern of light, shade, texture, not unlike the pattern set up by the repeated tractors in the
107   Stenbergs' *To the Fallow Ground*. Moholy-Nagy's emphasis on repetition as a formal device uniquely available to photomontage is really the reverse of that quality of photomontage explored by the Dadaists and Heartfield – its capacity for expressing oppositions, for dialectics. While not totally denuded of its representational qualities (the photograph is less incidental for him than it is, sometimes, in the work of
192, 194   graphic designers like Tschichold), the photographic image has become essential, not just added to the non–objective clarity of the composition.

154

194 Laszlo Moholy-Nagy *Jealousy*
1930

195 Laszlo Moholy-Nagy *The Shooting Gallery* 1925

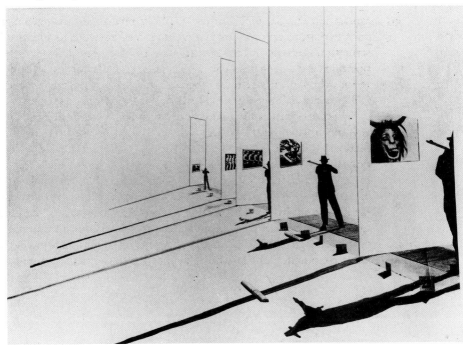

198-9   A number of De Stijl and International Constructivist artists also, for a variety of reasons, turned sometimes to photomontage. One of those whose use of photographic materials is most closely linked visually to his work in other mediums was Vordemberge-Gildewart, who made neo-plastic paintings, reliefs and collages as well as photomontages. In
196   *Untitled* (1928), he combines abstract pictorial elements with initially representational ones; the head of a chimpanzee is from a book of animal photographs by Paul Eipper, but has been turned upside down and altered by enclosure in dense, shiny, black paper.

    César Domela-Nieuwenhuis, on the other hand, who was also a De Stijl artist and has continued to paint and make reliefs and constructions, works of ordered and geometric abstraction, used in his photomontages photographs of industrial sites and details of machines, and, rather than disguising or subverting these, emphasized their impact and force by the use of powerful diagonals, contrasts of scale and angled
200 views. In *Energy*, a close-up of static electricity generators is combined with a steep perspective of industrial machinery. Domela and other colleagues collaborated to promote their work to companies and corporations for use in advertising campaigns. During the twenties and early thirties in particular numerous adventurous companies used work by radical young artists and designers (many incorporating photomon-
197 tages) such as Piet Zwart, Schuitema, Burchartz, Jan Tschichold.

★   ★   ★

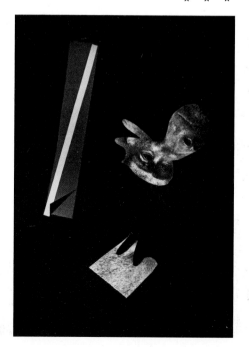

196 Friedrich Vordemberge-Gildewart *Untitled* 1928

197 Piet Zwart, advertising photomontage, 1931. Photomontage was increasingly utilized in advertising in the late 20s and 30s, often by artists whose 'studio work' was abstract

198 (*right*) Willi Baumeister *Head* 1923

199 (*below*) Hans Leistikov, photomontage reproduced in *Photo-Eye* 1929

200 César Domela-
Nieuwenhuis *Energy* 1931

201 (*opposite*) Tim Head
Equilibrium (Knife's Edge)
1976

Hausmann has been amply proved right since he wrote: 'The field of photomontage is so vast that it has as many possibilities as there are different milieux, and in its social structure and the resulting psychological superstructure the milieu changes every day. The possibilities of photomontage are limited only by the discipline of its formal means.'[5] Since Hausmann said this, in 1931, photographic processes have evolved, from everyman's Xerox to the sophisticated and expensive techniques of advertising, which are potential extensions and refinements of the genre. Many artists have taken advantage of the new reproductive processes to incorporate photographic material, like Andy Warhol, or Robert Rauschenberg. The silk-screen print, now often made photographically, can, as in Kitaj's *Addled Art*, combine photographs (and, in this case, a film still from Dali and Buñuel's *L'Age d'Or*).

203

This book has examined the historical origins of photomontage and suggested some predominant themes, their intersections and parallel developments. Today, probably the most familiar mode of photomontage is that of advertising. But the social and sexual constructions of advertising (whether or not using photomontage itself) may be revealed in their true nature by photomontage which uses advertising to expose hidden prejudices and assumptions. Such usage is not new: it goes back to Heartfield, to Dada and particularly to Hannah Höch. For instance, in her *Da-Dandy*, reproduced on the cover of this book, photographic fragments representing the pose, gaze, dress and ornament of woman in the context of fashion are recombined to form the outline of a man's head – defined by a thin red line – thus creating the sort of subversive ambiguity which is the central strategy of this form of art.

202 David Hockney *George, Blanche Celia Albert and Percy. London January 1983*

203 R. B. Kitaj *Addled Art* 1975

VOLUME VI

Minor
Works

EDITED

ÈRITD

Georges
BERNANOS

ADDLED
ART

MINOR
WORKS

ADDLED ART MINOR WORKS VOLUME VI

Notes

1 Introduction

1 For further examples see A. Jakovsky, *A Picture Postcard Album* (London, 1961), and Paul Eluard's marvellous collection 'Les plus belles cartes postales' in the Surrealist periodical *Minotaure*, no. 3–4, December 1933.
2 See Aaron Scharf, *Art and Photography* (London, 1974), p. 109.
3 Paul Hammond discusses the possible influence on Méliès of Albert Allis Hopkins's *Magic, Stage Illusions and Scientific Diversions, Including Trick Photography* (1897), which 'provided a convenient resume of contemporary photographic trickery', in his *Marvellous Méliès* (London, 1974).
4 Raoul Hausmann, *Courrier Dada* (Paris, 1958), p. 42 (author's translation). The dispute over the 'discovery' of photomontage is discussed in more detail in the next chapter.
5 It is curious that Walter Benjamin who, in 'The Work of Art in the Age of Mechanical Reproduction' (1936) credits Dada with the 'destruction of the aura of their creations' through their use of valueless materials in their collages, and with an impulse to attain effects attainable 'only with a changed technical standard' – i.e., film – should not have noted the special effect of photomontage.
6 Quoted in Van Deren Coke, *The Painter and the Photograph* (Albuquerque, New Mexico, 1972), p. 259. Höch made a similar point in conversation with the author in 1977.
7 Louis Aragon, 'Max Ernst, peintre des illusions' in *Les Col-* lages (Paris, 1965), p. 29, author's translation.
8 Louis Aragon, 'La peinture au défi', op. cit. p. 44, author's translation.
9 William Rubin, *Dada, Surrealism and their Heritage* (Museum of Modern Art, New York, 1968), p. 42.
10 Sergei Tretyakov, *John Heartfield* (OGIS state publishing house, Moscow, 1936); quoted in *John Heartfield* (Arts Council catalogue, 1969).
11 Aaron Scharf, in a letter to the author.

2 The Supremacy of the Message

Dada in Berlin

1 Franz Roh, *Foto-Auge/Oeil et Photo/Photo-Eye* (Stuttgart, 1929), p. 18. This book was published to coincide with the Film und Foto Werkbund exhibition in Stuttgart, which included a number of more recent photomontages by Heartfield, as well as examples of photomontage in advertising. The book contained 76 'photos of the period', among them photomontages by Berlin and Cologne Dadaists, and Bauhaus photography.
2 Hans Richter, *Dada: Art and Anti-Art* (London, 1965), p. 117; first published in *Blätter des Piscatorbühne*, 1928.
3 Hausmann, op. cit. p. 42.
4 Richter, op. cit. p. 117.
5 Hannah Höch, exhibition catalogue, Musée d'Art Moderne de la Ville de Paris, 1976, p. 31.
6 This satirical-political paper, brought out by Wieland Herzfelde's publishing house, the Malik-Verlag, as the government of the new German Republic took office in Weimar, and banned as soon as it appeared on the streets, was not strictly speaking published under the Dada banner. The Malik-Verlag, founded during the First World War, published both Dada works and satirical-political reviews like *Jedermann . . ., Der Gegner, Die Pleite*. Grosz drawings and Grosz-Heartfield montages appeared in most of these publications.
7 See Herta Wescher, *Collage* (New York, 1968), p. 146.
8 Wescher (p. 145) speaks of one of the sheets of montage portraits for *Der Dada 3* containing a dedication from Grosz to 'Photomonteur R. Hausmann', and 'takes this as confirmation that Grosz acknowledged him to be the father of photomontage'.
9 See Hanne Bergius, 'Zu Wahrnehmung und Wahrnehmungskritik in Der Dadaistichen Phase von Grosz und Heartfield', in E. Siepmann, *Montage: John Heartfield* (Berlin, 1977).
10 Hausmann, op. cit. p. 46, author's translation.
11 Richard Huelsenbeck, 'En avant Dada' in Robert Motherwell (ed.), *Dada Painters and Poets* (New York, 1951), p. 40.
12 *The Daily Express* (21 April 1921) reported the trial as follows: 'Official Germany's lack of a sense of humour was well illustrated today in a trial in which "Chief Dada" and "World Dada", two of the leaders of the Dadaist movement in Germany, were accused of mocking Prussian militarism. 'The "Dada" cult, which takes its name from the first word babies speak, has made vast strides in Germany recently. An exhibition

in Berlin attracted much attention because of the caricatures of Prussian soldiers.'
13 Huelsenbeck, op. cit. p. 37
14 See John Elderfield, *Kurt Schwitters* (London, 1985), pp. 77–9.
15 George Grosz and Wieland Herzfelde, *Die Kunst ist in Gefahr* (Berlin, 1925).

Heartfield

16 Louis Aragon, 'John Heartfield et la beauté révolutionnaire', op. cit. p. 78, author's translation.
17 John Berger, *Selected Essays and Articles: The Look of Things* (London, 1972), p. 185.
18 Quoted in *John Heartfield* (Arts Council catalogue, 1969).

Propaganda, Publicity and Constructivism

19 Quoted in Szymon Bojko, *New Graphic Design in Revolutionary Russia* (London, 1972), p. 21.
20 Quoted in Hausmann, op. cit. p. 49, author's translation.
21 Vasilii Rakitin, 'Gustav Klucis: Between the Non-Objective World and World Revolution', *The Avant-Garde in Russia 1910–30: New Perspectives* (Los Angeles, 1980), p. 62. See also Christina Lodder, *Russian Constructivism* (New Haven, 1983), p. 296, note 42.
22 See Ades, 'Dada-Constructivism', *Dada-Constructivism* (London, 1984), p. 43.
23 See Hubertus Gassner, 'La construction de l'Utopie: photomontages en URSS 1919–42', *Utopies et Réalités en URSS 1917–34*, p. 51, for a comparison between Klutsis and Rodchenko.
24 See Rowell and Rudenstine, *Art of the Avant-Garde in Russia; Selections from the George Costakis Collection* (Solomon R. Guggenheim Museum, New York, 1981), pp. 188–9); Lodder, op. cit. pp. 186–91 and 296. Lodder slightly misunderstands my argument in claiming that I imply photomontage appeared under the aegis of *Lef*. What I argued in the original edition, as I do here, was that the early date Klutsis gave his first photomontages was in all probability correct but that photomontage gathered momentum in 1923.
25 'Unovis': 'Affirmers of the New Art'.
26 Quoted by Bojko, op. cit. p. 30. Written on the back of a photograph of *Dynamic City*, in Klutsis's hand, is the following: 'no. 5, 1919. The last stage of abstract art and the emergence of a new type of representation. A photograph is used here as factual material. This ended abstract art. From this point we can identify the beginning of photomontage in the USSR. It was a kind of graphic art for agitprop. It is used extensively in literature for the masses and political posters.' My thanks to Kenneth Archer for providing me with this translation.
27 Kasimir Malevich, 'Aux Novateurs de l'univers tout entier' (1919), in *Arts et Poésies Russes 1910–30* (Paris, 1979), author's translation.
28 The theme of sport was continued in a series of photomontage postcards in 1928.
29 See Bojko, op. cit. p. 30.
30 El Lissitzky, 'Ideological Superstructures' from *Neues Bauen in der Welt: Russland* (1930); reprinted in Sophie Lissitzky-Küppers, *El Lissitzky* (London, 1968), p. 371.
31 *Lef*, no. 4, 1924, p. 41, translation Michael Skinner, 1985.
32 Osip Brik, 'From Pictures to Textile Prints' (1924), translated in J. E. Bowlt, ed., *Russian Art of the Avant-Garde: Theory and Criticism 1902-1934* (New York, 1976).
33 All quotations are from *Mayakovsky*, translated and edited by Herbert Marshall (London, 1965).
34 El Lissitzky, 'Our Book' (1926) in Lissitzky-Küppers, op. cit. p. 359.
35 *Lef*, no. 1, March 1923.
36 Kuleshov, 'The principles of montage' (1935) in Levaco (ed.), *Kuleshov on Film* (Berkeley, 1974), p. 194.
37 Quoted by Alma Law, 'The Russian Film Poster 1920–30', in Ades, *The 20th Century Poster: Design of the Avant-Garde* (Minneapolis and New York, 1984), p. 80.
38 See *Women Artists of the Russian Avante-Garde 1910–30* (Cologne, 1980) and *Kunst in die Produktion* (Berlin, 1977).
39 S. Kirsanov, quoted in Bojko, op. cit. p. 37.

3 Metropolis: The Vision of the Future

1 F. T. Marinetti, *The Founding and Manifesto of Futurism*, 1909, in Apollonio, *Futurist Manifestos* (London, 1973), p. 22.
2 El Lissitzky, 'A. and Pangeometry' from *Europa-Almanach* (1925); reprinted in Lissitzky-Küppers, op. cit. p. 348.
3 Jacques Ohayon, 'Malevitch. Le degré zéro de l'architecture', *Malevitch: Architectones Peintures Dessins* (Centre Georges Pompidou, Paris, 1980), p. 24.
4 I am indebted to Nicholas Boyarsky for pointing this out.

4 The Marvellous and the Commonplace

1 Elderfield, op. cit. pp. 79–80.
2 Max Ernst, *Beyond Painting* (New York, 1948), p. 14.
3 André Breton, *Le Surréalisme et la peinture* (Paris, 1928); translated by Simon Watson-Taylor, *Surrealism and Painting* (New York and London, 1972), p. 26.
4 Letter from Max Ernst to Tristan Tzara, 17 February 1920, in *Max Ernst* (Grand Palais exhibition catalogue, Paris, 1975).
5 Breton, preface to the Max Ernst exhibition, Paris, May 1921, in Ernst, op. cit. p. 177.
6 Breton, *Surrealism and Painting*, p. 27.
7 Ibid. p. 32.

163

8 Paul Nash, 'The Life of the inanimate object' in *Country Life*, May 1937, p. 57.
9 In *Architectural Review*, April 1936, pp. 151–4.
10 From commentary in *View*, March 1945, by 'Cpl Peter Lindamood'.
11 Susan Sontag, 'Melancholy Objects', *On Photography* (London, 1979), p. 52.

12 See Breton, 'Introduction to the Discourse on the Paucity of Reality', translated in Rosemont (ed.), *What is Surrealism?* (London, 1978) pp. 22–3.

5 Photomontage and Non-Objective Art

1 Quoted in Richard Kostalanetz (ed.), *Moholy-Nagy* (New York, 1970), p. 57.

2 Moholy-Nagy, *Painting Photography Film* (Bauhaus Book no. 8, reprinted London, 1969).
3 Moholy-Nagy, 'Space, time and the photographer' in Kostalanetz, op. cit. p. 65.
4 Moholy-Nagy, 'A new instrument of vision' in Kostalanetz, op. cit. p. 50.
5 Hausmann, op. cit. p. 48, author's translation.

List of Illustrations

Measurements are in centimetres, height before width

1 George Grosz (1893–1959), *Heartfield the Mechanic*, 1920. Watercolour and collage of pasted postcard and halftone 41.9 × 30.5. Collection Museum of Modern Art, New York. Gift of A. Conger Goodyear.
Heartfield changed his name from Herzfelde during World War I, as an anti-nationalistic gesture and as witness to the admiration he shared at the time with Grosz for all things American. Grosz has said that, at the time when he and Heartfield were inventing photomontage, they were receiving American picture magazines which contained a lot of photographic material.

2 W. Fox Talbot (1800–77), photogenic drawing, *c.* 1835. Lacock Abbey Collection.

3 German postcard, *c.* 1902. Photomontage 13.6 × 8.8. Altonaer Museum, Hamburg.

4 *A Fine Trio*, 1914. Photomontage postcard 13.7 × 9.2. Altonaer Museum, Hamburg.

5 John P. Morrissey, composite photograph, 1896. From Fraprie and Woodbury, *Photographic Amusements*, Boston, 1931.

6 Oscar G. Rejlander (1813–75), *The Two Ways of Life*, 1857. Photomontage, 40.6 × 78.7. Royal Photographic Society, London.
This large allegorical combination print was bought by Queen Victoria.

7, 8a, 8b Henry Peach Robinson (1830–1901), *Nor'Easter*. Combination printing. From Robinson, *Art Photography*, London, 1890.

9 Georges Méliès (1861–1938), still from *The Man With the Rubber Head*, 1902. Photo courtesy National Film Archive, London.

10 Raoul Hausmann (1886–1971), *Double Portrait: Hausmann-Baader*, 1920. Photomontage 25.4 × 15.8. Photo courtesy Galleria Schwarz, Milan.

11 Advertisement page for *Novy Lef*, Moscow, 1927.

12 René Magritte (1898–1967), *I Do Not See the (Woman) Hidden in the Forest*, from *La Révolution Surréaliste*, no. 12, Paris, 1929.

13 Pierre Boucher, photomontage. From Marcel Natkin, *Fascinating Fakes in Photography*, London, 1939.

14 Hannah Höch (1889–1978), *Cut with the Cake-Knife*, *c.* 1919. Collage 114 × 89.8. Nationalgalerie, Staatliche Museen Preussischer Kulturbesitz, Berlin.
The central quotation at the bottom of the picture reads: 'Cut with the cake-knife of Dada through the last beer-swilling cultural epoch of the Weimar Republic.'
The title of this work is in fact ambiguous: it is impossible to tell on the original work whether it is 'küchen' or 'kuchen' – kitchen or cake-knife. Ger-

trude Jula Dech's *Schnitt mit dem Küchenmesser DADA*, Berlin, 1981, gives a full account of the work and its title variants.

15 *Germany's Safeguard*, 1913. Photomontage. Altonaer Museum, Hamburg.

16 Hannah Höch (1889–1978), *Dada-Ernst*, 1920-1. Collage 18.6 × 16.6. Photo courtesy Galleria Schwarz, Milan.

17 Hannah Höch (1889–1978), *Collage*, 1920. Morton G. Neumann Family Collection.

18 John Heartfield (1891–1968), *Neue Jugend*, no. 2, June 1917.

19 John Heartfield (1891–1968), cover of *Jedermann sein eigner Fussball*, no. 1, 15 February 1919. Photomontage.

The first of the post-war satirical periodicals produced by the Malik-Verlag, *Jedermann* was banned after the first issue.

20 George Grosz (1893–1959) and John Heartfield (1891-1968), *Dada-merika*, 1919. Photomontage 29 × 19. Collection Paul Citroën. Photo Prentenkabinet, Rijksuniversiteit te Leiden.

21 John Heartfield (1891–1968), cover for *Der Dada 3*, Berlin, April 1920.

22 Johannes Baader (1876–1955), *Dada Milchstrasse*, 1918–20. 50 × 32.5. Photo courtesy Galleria Schwarz, Milan. This work includes the photomontage joint portrait of Baader and Hausmann with Baader's pipe 'smoking' a rose, which was reproduced in *Der Dada 2*, Berlin, December 1919.

23 Page from the trial proofs of the unpublished anthology *Dadaco*, 1920 (issued in facsimile, Milan, 1970)

24 George Grosz (1893–1968), *My Germany*, 1919. Trial proof for unpublished anthology *Dadaco*, 1920.

25 Hausmann and Höch at the International Dada Fair, Berlin, 1920. Photograph.

26 Raoul Hausmann (1886–1971), *Dada Conquers (Dada siegt)*, 1920. Collage. Photo courtesy Verlag M. Dumont Schauberg, Cologne.

27 Raoul Hausmann (1886–1971), *Tatlin at Home*, 1920. Collage of pasted papers and gouache 40.9 × 27.9. Photo Moderna Museet, Stockholm.

28 Raoul Hausmann (1886-1971), *The Spirit of Our Time – Mechanical Head*, 1919. Wood, metal, leather and cardboard, height 32.5. Musée National d'Art Moderne, Paris. Photo Musées Nationaux.

This work was reproduced for the first time in *Mecano* (Blue number), Leiden, 1922.

29 *Dada Almanach* cover, Berlin, 1920. Photomontage. Photo Eric Pollitzer.

30 George Grosz (1893-1959) and John Heartfield (1891-1968), *Life and Activity in Universal City at 12.05 midday*, 1919. Photomontage. Photo Akademie der Künste der DDR, Berlin.

31 Hannah Höch (1889–1978), *Dada-Dance*, 1922. Collage 32 × 23. Photo courtesy Galleria Schwarz, Milan.

32 Erwin Blumenfeld (Bloomfield) (1897–1969), *Bloomfield President Dada-Chaplinist*, 1921. Collage 13.3 × 8.8. Photo courtesy Galleria Schwarz, Milan.

33 Kurt Schwitters (1887-1948), *Film*, 1926. Photomontage-collage 19 × 15. Photo courtesy Galleria Schwarz, Milan.

34 George Grosz (1893–1959) and John Heartfield (1891–1968), *Corrected Self-Portrait of Rousseau*, 1920. Photomontage. Photo Eric Pollitzer. The head of Henri Rousseau has been replaced by a picture of Hausmann.

35 Johannes Baader (1874–1955), *The Author in his Home*, 1920. Collage of pasted photographs on book page 21.4 × 14.5. Collection Museum of Modern Art, New York.

36 Raoul Hausmann (1886–1971), *The Art Critic*, 1919. Mixed media 31.4 × 25.1. Tate Gallery, London.

37 George Grosz (1893–1959), cover of *Ma*, Vienna, June 1921.

38 Heinz Hajek-Halke (b. 1898), *The Banjo Player*, c. 1930. Private collection. Hajek-Halke studied photography in Berlin during the 1920s and made his first montages in 1925.

39 Raoul Hausmann (1886–1971), *ABCD*, 1923–4. Collage of pasted papers 40.7 × 28.5. Sidney Janis Gallery, New York.

40 John Heartfield (1891–1968), *The Spirit of Geneva*, 27 November 1932. Photomontage.

41 Poster issued during the Spanish Civil War by the Republican propaganda ministry against the use

of Moorish troops. Photomontage. Kunstgewerbe-museum, Zürich.

42 Poster issued by Republican ministry of prop-aganda during Spanish Civil War. Photomontage. Victoria and Albert Museum.

43 John Heartfield (1891–1968), cover for Upton Sinclair, *After the Flood*, Berlin, 1925. Photomontage. Photo Akademie der Künste der DDR, Berlin.

44 John Heartfield (1891–1968), endpapers for J. Dorfmann, *Im Land des Rekordzahlen*, 1927. Photo-montage 19.6 × 25. Photo courtesy Galleria Schwarz, Milan.

45 John Heartfield (1891–1968), *A Pan-German*, 2 November 1933. Photomontage. Photo Akademie der Künste der DDR, Berlin.

46 Stuttgart police photograph. From Franz Roh, *Foto-Auge*, 1929.

47 John Heartfield (1891–1968), *The Finest Products of Capitalism*, March 1932. Photomontage.

48 John Heartfield (1891–1968), *Hymn to the Forces of Yesterday: we pray to the might of the bomb*, 12 April 1934. Photomontage. Photo Akademie der Künste der DDR, Berlin.
The bombs forming the cathedral are labelled with the names of firms involved in armaments manufac-ture. The text reads: 'If you want armaments com-missions, then finance peace conferences/The choir of the armaments industry: "Geneva is our refuge and our strength."'

49 John Heartfield (1891–1968), *The Sleeping Reich-stag*, 1929. Photomontage from Kurt Tucholsky, *Deutschland, Deutschland Uber Alles*, Berlin, 1929. Photo Akademie der Künste der DDR, Berlin.

50 John Heartfield (1891–1968), *Goering the Execu-tioner*, 14 September 1933. Photomontage. Photo Akademie der Künste der DDR, Berlin.

51 John Heartfield (1891–1968), *Through Light to Night*, 19 May 1933. Photomontage.

52 John Heartfield (1891–1968), *Justicia*, 30 November 1933. Photomontage. Photo Akademie der Künste der DDR, Berlin.

53 John Heartfield (1891–1968), *Adolf the Superman* . . ., 17 July 1932. Photomontage.

54 John Heartfield (1891–1968), *The Suicide's Wish Fulfilment*. As originally published in *AIZ*, 26 September 1935, the text read: 'The little club foot's

wish fulfilment on the agitation speech of the propaganda minister Dr Goebbels against the Soviet Union on the Nuremberg Party Day'.

55 Xanti (Alexander Schawinsky) (b. 1907), *Musso-lini*, 1934.

56 Voskuil, poster for exhibition on Olympics under Nazi patronage, 1936. Photomontage. Stedelijk Museum, Amsterdam.

57 John Heartfield (1891–1968), *The Crisis Party Convention...*, 15 June 1931. Photomontage (photo-gravure) 35.2 × 26. Collection Museum of Modern Art, New York.

58 John Heartfield (1891–1968), *Herr von Papen on the Hunting Path*, 11 October 1934. Photomontage. Photo Akademie der Künste der DDR, Berlin.

59 John Heartfield (1891–1968), *Millions Stand Be-hind Me*, 16 October 1932. Photomontage. Photo Akademie der Künste der DDR, Berlin.

60 John Heartfield (1891–1968), *German Natural History: Metamorphosis*, 16 August 1934. Photomon-tage, Photo Akademie der Künste der DDR, Berlin. The additional text from *AIZ* reads:
German Death's Head Moth (Acherontia atropos germanica) in its three stages of development: cater-pillar, pupa and moth. Metamorphosis means: 1. in mythology: the transformation of human beings into trees, animals, rocks, etc. 2. In zoology: the de-velopment of various creatures through larval forms and pupae, for example caterpillar, pupa, butterfly. 3. In the history of the Weimar Republic: the direct progression EBERT (1919–25) – HINDENBURG (1925–34) – HITLER (1934–45).

61 John Heartfield (1891–1968), *WAR: Sudeten Germans, you'll be the first!* 13 September 1938. Photo-montage. Photo Akademie der Künste der DDR, Berlin. On 29 September 1938, Chamberlain, Dala-dier, Hitler and Mussolini met in Munich and reached agreement on the annexation of Sudetenland by Germany.

62 John Heartfield (1891–1968), *Hurrah, the Butter is Finished!* 19 December 1935. Photomontage. Photo Akademie der Künste der DDR, Berlin.

63 John Heartfield (1891–1968), Manifesto of Span-ish Communist Party published by Central Com-mittee, Barcelona. Photomontage. Canning House Library, London.

64 *Private Eye* cover, March 1966. Photomontage.

Photo courtesy *Private Eye*.

65　David King (b. 1943), *A Short Sharp Shock*, 1980. Photomontage. Collection the artist.

66　Red Dragon Print Collective, *Control* poster for Radical Alternatives to Prison, 1975. Photomontage 51 × 33. Photo courtesy Red Dragon Print Collective.

67　Peter Kennard (b. 1949), *Haywain with Cruise Missiles*, 1983, from GLC Peace Poster portfolio. Collection the artist.

68　Peter Kennard (b. 1949), *Defended to Death*, 1982, from GLC Peace Poster portfolio. Collection the artist.

69　El Lissitzky (1890–1941), poster for the Exhibition of Soviet Art, Zürich, 1929. Photomontage. Collection Museum of Modern Art, New York. Gift of Philip Johnson.

70　El Lissitzky (1890–1941) and Sergey Senkin (1894–1963), *The Task of the Press is the Education of the Masses*. Photographic frieze for International Press Exhibition, Cologne, 1928. From Szymon Bojko, *New Graphic Design in Revoluntionary Russia*, Lund Humphries, London, 1972.
The huge mural montage of photographs celebrated the achievements of the Revolution. Other artists such as Klutsis and Kulagina also worked on the Soviet Pavilion at this Exhibition.

71　Entrance to Soviet Pavilion, International Hygiene Exhibition, Dresden, 1930. Photomontages and photographs. Photo courtesy VEB Verlag der Kunst, Dresden.

72　Varvara Stepanova (1894–1958), illustration from the album *Gaust Tschaba*, 1919. Collage on newsprint 17.5 × 27.5. Photo Galerie Gmurzynska, Cologne.

73　Gustav Klutsis (1895–1944), *The Old World and The World being built Anew*, 1920. Photomontage. State Museum of Mayakovsky, Moscow.

74　Gustav Klutsis (1895–1944), *Dynamic City*, 1919–21. Photomontage. State Art Museum of Latvia, Riga.

75　Gustav Klutsis (1895–1944), *Dymanic City*, 1919–21. Oil with sand and concrete on wood 87 × 64.5. © 1981 George Costakis. The George Costakis Collection (Owned by Art Co. Ltd).

76　Gustav Klutsis (1895–1944), *Sport*, 1922. Photo-

montage. Photo courtesy Verlag M. Dumont Schauberg, Cologne.

77　Gustav Klutsis (1895–1944), *The Electrification of the Entire Country*, 1920. Photomontage. State Museum of Mayakovsky, Moscow.

78　Sergey Senkin (1894–1963), photomontage for a special edition of *Molodaya gwardya* (to Lenin), 1924. From Bojko, op. cit.

79　Gustav Klutsis (1895–1944), as pl. 78. From Bojko, op. cit.

80　El Lissitzky (studio), *The Lenin Podium*, 1924 (based on a sketch of 1920). Drawing with photomontage.

81　Juryi Roshkov, photomontage for Mayakovsky's poem 'A temporary monument...', *c.* 1925. From Bojko, op. cit.

82　Alexander Rodchenko (1891–1956), *The Crisis*, 1923. Photomontage. From Bojko, op. cit.

83　Gustav Klutsis (1895–1944), poster for an anti-imperialist exhibition, 1931. Photomontage. From Bojko, op. cit.

84　Russian poster marking the 14th anniversary of the Revolution, 1931. Photomontage. Kunstgewerbemuseum, Zürich.
Part of the text reads: 'Our greeting to the workers in the colonies, who are the prisoners of imperialism....'

85　Liubov Popova (1889–1924), documentary photograph of set design for *Zemila Dybom*, 1923. © 1981 George Costakis. The George Costakis Collection (Owned by Art Co. Ltd).

86　Gustav Klutsis (1895–1944), *The Struggle for the Bolshevik Harvest is the Struggle for Socialism* from the *Struggle for the Five-Year Plan* series of posters, 1931. Photomontage.

87　Gustav Klutsis (1895–1944), *Transport Achievement of the First Five-Year Plan*, 1929. Photomontage. Collection Museum of Modern Art, New York.
Klutsis's celebration of railway construction has similarities with Viktor Turin's film *Turksib*, on the building of the Turkestan-Siberia railway, which also juxtaposes the old method of transport (camel) with the new.

88–95　Alexander Rodchenko (1891–1956), photomontages for Mayakovsky's poem *About This*, 1923. By permission of the British Library Board.

96 El Lissitzky (1890–1941), photomontage, 1931. Photo Novosti Press Agency.

97, 98 Alexander Rodchenko (1891–1956), two standard cover designs for a series of detective stories, 1924, Photomontage. From Bojko, op. cit.

99 El Lissitzky (1890–1941), cover for Richard Neutra, *Amerika*, Anton Schroll, Vienna, 1929. Photomontage. Photo courtesy VEB Verlag der Kunst, Dresden.

100 Solomon Telingater (1903–69), photomontage for I. Feinberg, *The Year 1914*, 1934. From Bojko. op. cit.

101 El Lissitzky (1890–1941), cover of catalogue to Japanese Cinema Exhibition, Moscow, 1929 (detail). Photomontage. Photo Novosti Press Agency.

102 Sergei Eisenstein (1898–1948), still from *Strike*, 1924. Photo courtesy National Film Archive, London.

103 Dziga Vertov (1896–1954), still from *Man with a Movie Camera*, 1928. Photo courtesy National Film Archive, London.

104 Boris Prusakov, *I Hurry to see the Khaz Push*, 1927. Offset lithograph 71.1 × 105.4. Collection Museum of Modern Art, New York.

105 Alexander Rodchenko (1891–1956), poster for *Kino-Eye* directed by Dziga Vertov, 1924. Photo courtesy National Film Archive, London.

106 Vladimir (b. 1899) and Georgii (1900–33) Stenberg, poster for *The Eleventh*, directed by Dziga Vertov, 1928. Photo courtesy National Film Archive, London.

107 Vladimir (b. 1899) and Georgii (1900–33) Stenberg, *To the Fallow Ground*, 1928. Photomontage. From Bojko. op. cit.

108 Mieczyslaw Szczuka (1898–1927), *Kemal's Constructive Program*, 1924. Photomontage. Photo courtesy Muzeum Sztuki, Lodz.

109 John Heartfield (1981–1968), *Liberty Fights in their Ranks* (after Delacroix), 19 August 1936. Photomontage.

110 Mieczyslaw Berman (b. 1903), *The Red Cap* (After Delacroix), 1969. Photocollage 40 × 29. Photo courtesy Galleria Schwarz, Milan.

111 A. Sitomirski (b. 1907), *Here's the Corporal ...*, 1941. Photomontage. Photo courtesy Verlag M.

Dumont Schauberg, Cologne. Sitomirski was a pupil of Heartfield; his satirical photomontages occasionally appeared in the magazine *Soviet Union*.

112 Mieczyslaw Berman (b. 1903), *Construction I*, 1927. Photomontage 57 × 36.5. Photo courtesy Galleria Schwarz, Milan.

113 El Lissitzky (1890–1941), montage from *USSR in Construction*, no. 10, 1932, Moscow. Photo courtesy VEB Verlag der Kunst, Dresden.

114 Gustav Klutsis (1895–1944), *Youth – Into the Air!* 1934. Photomontage. Poster.

115 Mieczyslaw Berman (b. 1903), *Lindbergh*, 1927. Photomontage 70 × 50. Photo courtesy Galleria Schwarz, Milan.

116 Valentina Kulagina (b. 1902, died 1930s), poster for the *International Women's Day* or *Women Workers, Shock Workers, Strengthen your Shock Brigades*, 1930. Photo Galerie Gmurzynska, Cologne.

117 Paul Citroën (b. 1896), *Metropolis*, 1923. Collage of photographs, prints and postcards 76.1 × 58.4. Prentenkabinet, Rijksuniversiteit te Leiden.

118 Otto Umbehr (Umbo) (1902–80), *Perspective of the Street*, 1926. Photograph (silverprint) 17.8 × 12.8. Photo courtesy Sotheby's. Private collection.

119 Walther Ruttmann (1887–1941), publicity material for the film *Berlin*, 1927. Photomontage. Photo courtesy National Film Archive, London.

120 Kazimierz Podsadecki (1904–70), *Modern City: melting pot of life*, 1928. Photomontage 43 × 29. Museum Sztuki, Lodz. From 1928 Podsadecki published a number of photomontages with a strong element of fantasy in various Polish illustrated weeklies. He was also a graphic designer and abstract painter.

121 Fritz Lang (b. 1890), montage of scenes from *Metropolis*, 1926. Photo courtesy National Film Archive, London.

122 Fritz Lang (b. 1890), still from *Metropolis*, 1926. Photo courtesy National Film Archive, London.

123 P. M. Bardi (b. 1900), *Panel of Horrors*, 1931. Photomontage. Photo courtesy Verlag M. Dumont Schauberg, Cologne.

124 César Domela-Nieuwenhuis (b. 1900), *Berlin Museums*, 1931. Photomontage mural for 'Fotomontage' exhibition in Kunstgewerbemuseum, Berlin, 1931.

125 Paul Citroën (b. 1896), *Brotenfeld*, 1928. Photocollage 25.5 × 32.5. Photo courtesy Galleria Schwarz, Milan.

126 Kazimir Malevich (1878–1935), *Project for a Suprematist Skyscraper for New York City*, 1926.

127 El Lissitzky (1890–1941), *Wolkenbügel*, Photomontage. Photo courtesy VEB Verlag der Kunst, Dresden.

128 Bohdan Lachert (b. 1900) and Jozef Szanajca (1902–39), *Design and Construction of a House, Warsaw*, 1928. Photomontage. Photo courtesy Muzeum Sztuki, Lodz.

129 Gyula Halasz Brassaï (1899–1984), *Ciel Postiche*, 1935, from *Minotaure*, no. 6, Paris, 1934/5.

130 German postcard, *c.* 1914. Photomontage 13.5 × 8.8. Altonaer Museum, Hamburg.

131 Postcard of Piccadilly Circus as Venice, *c.* 1905. Photomontage 9.6 × 14.3. Collection Aaron Scharf.

132 Louise Ernst-Strauss, *Augustine Thomas and Otto Flake*, 1920. Collage 23.1 × 13.4. Kestner-Museum, Hanover.

133 Francis Picabia (1879–1953), *Tableau Rastadada*, 1920. Photomontage. Photo courtesy Verlag M. Dumont Schauberg, Cologne.

134 Théodore Fraenkel, *Artistique et sentimental*, 1921. Collage 37 × 23.5. Photo courtesy Galleria Schwarz, Milan.

135 Kurt Schwitters (1887–1948), *Mz 158 The Kots Picture*, 1920. Collage 27 × 19.5. Sprengel Museum, Hanover.

136 Max Ernst (1891–1976), *Here Everything is Still Floating*, 1920. Collage of printed photographs with pencil on paper 10.5 × 12. Collection Museum of Modern Art, New York.
One of the 'Fatagagas' executed in Cologne, possibly with Arp's collaboration.

137 Max Ernst (1891–1976), *The Song of the Flesh*, 1920. Collage of photographs, gouache and pencil on cardboard 12 × 21. Private collection, Paris.
The hand-written text round the original reads: 'Le chien qui chie le chien bien coiffé malgré les difficultés du terrain causées par/une neige abondante la femme à belle gorge la chanson de la chair.'

138 Max Ernst (1891–1976), *Health Through Sport*, *c.* 1920. Photograph of a photomontage on a wood

support 101.5 × 59.8. Menil Foundation, Houston, Texas.

139 André Breton (1896–1966), *Automatic Writing*, 1938. Photomontage 14.2 × 10. Photo courtesy Galleria Schwarz, Milan.

140 Max Ernst (1891–1976), *The Punching Ball* or *Max Ernst and Caesar Buonarotti*, 1920. Collage, photographs and gouache on paper 17.6 × 11.5. Private collection.
Ernst here measures himself against Michelangelo.

141 Max Ernst (1891–1976), *Untitled* or *The Murderous Aeroplane*, 1920. Collage of photographs on paper 5.8 × 14.3. Private collection, USA.

142 Max Ernst (1891–1976), *The Chinese Nightingale*, 1920. Photomontage with Indian ink 14 × 10. Private collection.

143 Man Ray (b. 1890), self-portrait from *Minotaure*, no. 3–4, December 1933, Paris.

144 Albert Valentin (1908–68), photomontage, reproduced in *Variétés*, Brussels, 1929–30.

145 Eugene Atget (1856–1927), *Gentlemen's Fashions*. Photograph. Photo BBC Hulton Picture Library.

146 E. L. T. Mesens (1903–71), *The Disconcerting Light*, 1926. Private collection.

147 Max Ernst (1891–1976), *Loplop Introduces Members of the Surrealist Group*, 1930. Collage, photographs, frottage and crayon on paper 50 × 34. Collection Museum of Modern Art, New York.

148 André Breton (1896–1966) *The Serpent*, 1932. Photomontage 18 × 11. Photo courtesy Galleria Schwarz, Milan.

149 Paul Nash (1899–1946), *Swanage*, *c.* 1936. Photograph and drawing 40 × 58.1 Tate Gallery, London.
For a full description of the found objects of which Nash used photographs for this work, see *The Tate Gallery 1972-4*, 1975.

150 Roger Leigh (b. 1925), *Sarsens or Grey Wethers*, 1974. Photomontage triptych 48 × 75. Courtesy the artist.
Using 30 separate enlargement printings, this photomontage explores the relationship between sarsens, the standing grey stones of Wiltshire, and the hill sheep. It includes real objects, and the side panels slide together.

151 Marcel Mariën (b. 1920), *The Torrents of Spring*, 1966. Hair and tap. Photo Marcel Mariën.

152 Marcel Mariën (b. 1920), *Incest*, 1968. Photomontage from *Crystal Blinkers* (transl. J. Lyle), Transformaction, Harpford, Devon, 1973, one of the best recent Surrealist publications, which contains photographs, photomontages, collages, writings and other works by Mariën.

153 Kazimierz Podsadecki (1904–70), *Hands Speak*, 1931. Photomontage 39.2 × 28. Muzeum Sztuki, Lodz.

154 Marcel Duchamp (1887–1968), cover of *View*, March 1945, New York.

155 Friedrich Kiesler, *Les larves d'imagie d' Henri Robert Marcel Duchamp*, 1945. Folding photographic triptych. From *View* V, no. 1, March 1945 (Duchamp issue), New York.

156 Marcel Duchamp (1887–1968), *Family Portrait, 1899*, 1964.Photomontage 34 × 27. Photo courtesy Galleria Schwarz, Milan.
Duchamp has blotted himself out of the picture with a black shape paralleled by the shape enclosing the whole photograph.

157 Hannah Höch (1889–1978), From the collection: *From an Ethnographic Museum*, 1929. Collage 25.6 × 17. Private collection. Photo courtesy Annely Juda Fine Art, London.

158 Raoul Hausmann (1887–1971), photomontage, 1947. From Raoul Hausmann and Kurt Schwitters, *Pin*, 1962, London.

159 Hannah Höch (1889–1978), *Foreign Beauty*, 1929. Collage 32 × 23. Photo courtesy Galleria Schwarz, Milan.

160 Max Ernst (1891–1976), *Les Pléiades*, 1921. Collage of photographs, gouache and oil 24.5 × 16.5. Private collection.

161 Pierre Molinier (1900–76), *Les Hanel 2*, 1928. Photomontage for *Le Chaman et ses Créatures* by Roland Villeneuve. Photo courtesy Roger Cardinal.

162 Johannes Baargeld (1891–1927), *Venus and the Game of the Kings*, 1920. Collage 37 × 27.5. Photo courtesy Galliera Schwarz, Milan.

163 Frederick Sommer (b. 1905), *Max Ernst*, 1946. Collection the artist.

164 Raoul Ubac (b. 1909), *Penthesilia*, 1937 from *Minotaure*, no. 10, Winter, 1937, Paris.

165 Georges Hugnet (1906–74), *Untitled*, 1936. Collection Timothy Baum, New York.

166 Joseph Cornell (b. 1903), *Untitled* (Breton collage), 1966. Photocollage 40.6 × 31.7. Collection Susan Sontag.

167 René Magritte (1898–1967), *Paris Opera*, 1929, from *La Révolution Surréaliste*, no. 12, Paris, 1929. Detroit Institute of Art, Founders Society Purchase.

168 Florence Henri (1895–1982), *Abstract Composition*, 1932, Photomontage. Courtesy Martini and Ronchetti, Genoa.

169 Herbert Bayer (b. 1900), *The Language of Letters*, 1931. Photomontage 43.2 × 33. Courtesy Marlborough Gallery, London.

170 Jerry Uelsmann (b. 1934), *Untitled*, 1984. Collection the artist.

171 Herbert Bayer (b. 1900), *Lonely Metropolitan*, 1932. Photomontage 43.2 × 33. Courtesy Marlborough Gallery, London.

172 Maurice Tabard (1897–1984), *Hand and Woman*, 1929. Collection of Robert Shapazian, Fresno, California. Photo Corcoran Gallery, Washington.

173 Eduardo Paolozzi (b. 1924), *Collage over African Sculpture*, 1960. 25.5 × 14.9. Courtesy Anthony d'Offay Gallery.

174 Nigel Henderson (b. 1917), *Head of a Man*, 1956. Photographs on board. Tate Gallery, London.

175 Jacques Brunius (1906–67), *Ad Nauseam*, 1944. Collage. Photo courtesy Verlag M. Dumont Schauberg, Cologne.
Primarily a writer, Brunius left France in 1940 for England where, with E. L. T. Mesens, he helped to spread Surrealist ideas.

176 Penny Slinger (b. 1947), *The Abysmal*, 1975. From *An Exorcism*. Photomontage 38.1 × 45.7. Courtesy the artist.

177 Jerry Uelsmann (b. 1934), *Untitled*, 1983. Collection the artist.

178 Jordi Cerdà (b. 1949), *Suite Freud-Lacon*, 1983. Photomontage with collage and painting 80 × 100. The Suite consists of five works. Collection the artist.

179 Conroy Maddox (b. 1920), *Uncertainty of the Day*, 1940. Collage of photographs and gouache 14.9

× 20. Collection the artist. Photo courtesy Verlag M. Dumont Schauberg.

180 Lajos Kassak (1887-1967), *The Raven*, 1924. Collage 29 × 39. Photo courtesy Galleria Schwarz, Milan.
  In 1917, with others including Moholy-Nagy, Kassak organized an artists' group, *Ma*, and edited a magazine of the same name, first from Budapest and then from Vienna, where he was forced to emigrate following the collapse of the Communist government in Hungary. After early contacts with Dada, his work was influenced by Suprematism and Constructivism, but later he turned increasingly to Surrealism.

181 Terry Gilliam (b. 1940), photomontage for *Monty Python* TV series, 1971. Courtesy the artist. Photo BBC Copyright.

182 Richard Hamilton (b. 1922). *Just what is it ...*, 1956. Collage 26 × 24.8. Collection Erwin Janss, Jr., Thousand Oaks, California.

183 Laszlo Moholy-Nagy (1895-1946), *Structure of the World*, 1927. Photomontage. Photo International Museum of Photography at George Eastman House, Rochester.

184 Man Ray (b. 1890), *Rayogram: Kiki Drinking*, 1922. 23.8 × 17.8. From *The Age of Light: Photographs 1920-34*, Paris and New York, 1934.

185 Laszlo Moholy-Nagy (1895-1946), *Photogram: Lightening Rod*, 1940. Photo International Museum of Photography at George Eastman House, Rochester.

186 Herbert Bayer (b. 1900), cover of *Bauhaus I*, 1928. Photomontage. Bauhaus-Archiv, Berlin.
  In the 1930s, Bayer also used photomontage on the covers of the periodical *Die Neue Linie*.

187 Herbert Bayer (b. 1900), *Metamorphosis*, 1936. Photomontage 33 × 43.2. Courtesy Marlborough Gallery, London.

188 El Lissitzky (1890-1941), *The Constructor* (self-portrait), 1924. Photomontage. Photo courtesy VEB Verlag der Kunst, Dresden.

189 Kazimir Malevich (1878-1935), *Analytical Chart, c.* 1925. Collage with pencil on transparent paper, pen and ink 63.5 × 82.6. Collection Museum of Modern Art, New York.

190 Laszlo Moholy-Nagy (1895-1946), *Leda and the Swan*, 1925. Photomontage. Courtesy Galerie Klihm, Munich.

191 Christian Schad (b. 1894), *Schadograph*, 1918. Photogram 16.8 × 12.7. Collection Museum of Modern Art, New York. Purchase.
  Schad's experiments with 'cameraless photography' – the direct exposure of photo-sensitive paper to light – pre-date those of Man Ray and Moholy-Nagy; a *Schadograph* was reproduced in *Dadaphone* (*Dada*, no. 7) Paris, March 1920.

192 Laszlo Moholy-Nagy (1895-1946), *The Law of Series*, 1925. Photomontage 21.6 × 16.2. Collection Museum of Modern Art, New York. Given anonymously.

193 Jan Tschichold, poster for the film *Die Frau ohne Namen*, 1928. Photo courtesy Verlag M. Dumont Schauberg, Cologne.

194 Laszlo Moholy-Nagy (1895-1946), *Jealousy*, 1930. Photomontage. Photo International Museum of Photography at George Eastman House, Rochester.

195 Laszlo Moholy-Nagy (1895-1946), *The Shooting Gallery*, 1925. Photomontage. Courtesy Galerie Klihm, Munich.

196 Friedrich Vordemberge-Gildewart (1899-1962), *Untitled*, 1928. Collage and photomontage 40.3 × 28.9. Courtesy Marlborough Gallery, London.

197 Piet Zwart (b. 1885), advertisement for Nijgh en Van Ditmar, 1931. Photomontage 17.5 × 25. Collection Haags Gemeente-museum, The Hague.

198 Willi Baumeister (1889-1955), *Head*, 1923. Photocollage 35 × 24. Graphische Sammlung, Staatsgalerie, Stuttgart.

199 Hans Leistikov, photomontage reproduced in Franz Roh, *Photo-Eye*, Stuttgart, 1929.

200 César Domela-Nieuwenhuis (b. 1900), *Energy*, 1951. Photomontage 63.5 × 49. Courtesy Martini and Ronchetti, Genoa.

201 Tim Head (b. 1946), *Equilibrium (Knife's Edge)*, 1976. Photograph. Courtesy the artist.
  The use of the mirror disrupts the straight photograph to give the effect of photomontage.

202 David Hockney (b. 1937), *George, Blanche Celia Albert and Percy. London January 1983*.

203 R. B. Kitaj (b. 1932), *Addled Art*, 1975. Screenprint 105.1 × 71.1. Marlborough Graphics Ltd, London.

Selected Bibliography

ARAGON, Louis. *Les Collages.* Paris, 1965.

Arbeiterfotografie. Amsterdam and Berlin, 1978.

Art in Revolution. Arts Council of Great Britain, London, 1971.

BARRON, S., and TUCHMAN, M., eds. *The Avant-Garde in Russia 1910–30: New Perspectives.* Los Angeles Co. Museum of Art, 1980.

BERGER, John. *Selected Essays and Articles: The Look of Things.* London, 1972.

BOJKO, Szymon. *New Graphic Design in Revolutionary Russia.* London, 1972.

BRETON, André. *Surrealism and Painting.* Translated by Simon Watson-Taylor. New York and London, 1972.

Constructivism in Poland 1923–36: BLOK, Praesens, a.r. Museum Folkwang, Essen, and Rijksmuseum Kröller–Müller, Otterlo, 1973.

Dada and Surrealism Reviewed. Arts Council of Great Britain, London, 1978.

Dada Artifacts. The University of Iowa Museum of Art, Iowa City, 1978.

Dada Berlin: Texte, Manifeste, Aktionen. Bergius, H., and Riha, K., eds. Stuttgart, 1977.

Dada Photomontagen. Kestner Gesellschaft, Hanover, 1979.

Dada-Constructivism. Annely Juda Fine Art, London, 1984.

Der Dada. Berlin, 1919–20.

ELDERFIELD, John. *Kurt Schwitters.* London, 1985.

ERNST, Max. *Beyond Painting.* New York, 1948.

Film und Foto: Internationale Ausstellung des Deutschen Werkbunds. Stuttgart, 1929.

Film und Foto der Zwanzige Jahre. Stuttgart, 1979.

FOSTER, S., and KUENZLI, R., eds. *Dada Spectrum.* The University of Iowa, Iowa City, 1979.

GIROUD, Michel. *Raoul Hausmann 'Je ne suis pas un photographe'.* Paris, 1976.

GROSZ, George, and HERZFELDE, Wieland. *Die Kunst ist in Gefahr.* Berlin, 1925.

HANSER, Reihe. *John Heartfield: Krieg im Frieden. Fotomontagen 1930–38.* Munich, 1972.

HAUSMANN, Raoul. *Courrier Dada.* Paris, 1958.

HERZFELDE, Wieland. *John Heartfield.* Dresden, 1971.

HUELSENBECK, Richard. *Dada Almanach.* Berlin, 1920; New York, 1966.

JAGUER, Edouard. *Les Mystères de la Chambre Noire: Le Surréalisme et La Photographie.* Paris, 1982.

KOSTALANETZ, Richard. *Moholy-Nagy.* New York, 1970.

KRAUSS, R., and LIVINGSTONE, J. *L'Amour Fou: Photography and Surrealism* (with an essay by Dawn Ades). Washington and New York, 1985.

Kunst aus der Revolution. Neue Gesellschaft fur Bildende Kunst (NGBK), Berlin, with Staatlichen Tretjakov-Galerie, Moscow, 1977.

'Kunst in die Produktion!' NGBK, Berlin, 1977.

LISSITZKY-KÜPPERS, S. *El Lissitzky.* London, 1968, and Dresden, 1976.

LODDER, Christina. *Russian Constructivism.* New Haven, 1983.

MARTIN, J.-H. *Malevitch.* Centre Georges Pompidou, Paris, 1980.

MOHOLY-NAGY, Laszlo. *Painting Photography Film* (Bauhaus Book no. 8, 1925). London, 1969.

MOTHERWELL, Robert. *Dada Painters and Poets.* New York, 1951.

NATKIN, Marcel. *Fascinating Fakes in Photography.* London, 1939.

Paris–Berlin 1900–33. Centre Georges Pompidou, Paris, 1978.

Paris–Moscou 1900–30. Centre Georges Pompidou, Paris 1979.

RICHTER, Hans. *Dada: Art and Anti-Art.* London, 1965.

Rodchenko. Elliott, D., ed. Museum of Modern Art, Oxford, 1979.

ROH, Franz. *Photo-Eye.* Stuttgart, 1929.

RUBIN, William. *Dada and Surrealist Art.* London, 1969.

SCHARF, Aaron. *Art and Photography.* London, 1974.

SCHWARZ, Arturo, ed. *Almanacco Dada.* Milan, 1976.

SHEPPARD, Richard, ed. *New Studies in Dada: Essays and Documents.* Hutton, Humberside, 1981.

SIEPMANN, Eckhard. *Montage: John Heartfield.* Berlin, 1977.

SONTAG, Susan. *On Photography.* London, 1979.

Tendenzen Der Zwanzige Jahre. 15 Europaische Kunstausstellung, Berlin, 1977.

Utopies et Réalités en URSS 1917–34. Centre Georges Pompidou, Paris, 1980.

VAN DEREN COKE. *The Painter and the Photograph.* Albuquerque, New Mexico, 1972.

Wem Gehort die Welt – Kunst unde Gesellschaft in der Weimarer Republik. NGBK, Berlin, 1977.

Wescher, Herta. *Collage.* New York, 1968.

Index

Figures in *italic* refer to illustration numbers